WHY I
FAILED

WHY I FAILED
LESSONS FROM LEADERS

SHWETA PUNJ

RANDOM HOUSE INDIA

Published by Random House India in 2013

1

Copyright © Shweta Punj 2013

Random House Publishers India Private Limited
Windsor IT Park, 7th Floor
Tower-B, A-1, Sector-125
Noida 201301, UP

Random House Group Limited
20 Vauxhall Bridge Road
London SW1V 2SA
United Kingdom

978 81 8400 082 5

Typeset in GoudyOlSt BT by R. Ajith Kumar

Printed and bound in India by Replika Press Private Limited

To my grandparents, Surinder Mohan, Kaushalya Devi, and Bimla Mudgill—for their blessings and so much love

Contents

Contents

Introduction

'Failure, then, failure! So the world stamps us at every turn. We strew it with our blunders, our misdeeds, our lost opportunities, with all the memorials of our inadequacy to our vocation. And with what a damning emphasis does it then blot us out!'

—*William James*

Isn't the fear of failure a barrier that often holds us back from getting what we really want and becoming who we want to be? Why does failure feel so wrong? Unfair? Discouraging? Why does it hurt so much to fail? Why does failure seem like the end of the road? Failure can feel worse than death. Remember the '*Why didn't I just die?*' feeling? Certain failures can just kill us and many of them make us want to bite the dust.

It is no wonder then that there is so much written and said on how one could 'cope' with failure. It is unappetizing, nauseating, and difficult to digest. It is also a cultural thing.

In India, we look at failure with much disdain and discomfort. From the moment we step into the real world, so to speak, it is ingrained in us that we always have to succeed at everything. We *cannot* fail. History only applauds winners.

If we look at the chronological framework of India's history, it is about winners. The battles, the endowment of religious institutions, dates of inscriptions are there because people who were the 'winners', the powerful, believed those records were important to preserve. But as many historians have reiterated, all that we know of Indian history is not all that we could know. The historical records tell us more about the kings, the powerful, the winners.

It is surprising that the story of Sage Raikva (a homeless bullock cart driver) was quoted in the Upanishads—the text of the Brahmins. King Janusruti seeks the help of Raikva to win over his people. What is surprising here is not that Raikva helped the king win, but that he got a mention in the Upanishads which is largely about the Brahmin elite.

Usually failure is either impossible to remember or impossible to forget.

Sigmund Freud in the *Psychopathology of Everyday Life* recounts an experience: Once, while settling his monthly accounts, Freud came upon the name of a patient whose case history he couldn't recall, even though he could see that he had visited her every day for many weeks, just six months ago. He tried very hard to remember the patient, until the memory finally came back to him. The patient in question was a woman whose parents brought her in because she complained incessantly of stomach pains. Freud diagnosed her with hysteria. A few months later, she died of abdominal cancer.

Over the course of working on this book, when I would explain the topic to friends, family, or even senior executives of companies, most would respond by saying: 'Why failure? Why would you pick a topic like failure?' And that's exactly the reaction I was expecting and hoping for. Failure, much like success, is not for everyone.

This book is built around stories of people who screwed up, sometimes again and again. These stories involve imagination, miscalculations, illusions, misadventures, ambition, love affairs, inspiration, and most importantly courage.

Each story is revelatory at several levels, exploring failures of varying degrees and varieties—messing up on the first big opportunity, failing in coping with bureaucracy and nepotism, failure of life's circumstances, failing to lead and making others follow your vision—every chapter offers an insight into failure of a different kind.

Most often, the experience of recognizing failure can be life-altering, shocking, funny, pleasurable, cathartic, illuminating, and confusing. The realization process usually puts us at odds with ourselves. In the aftermath of failure, we question ourselves, our abilities:

'How could have I done that?'

'What was I even thinking?'

'Did I really do that?'

But, just for a moment, if you put the hurt, injury, insults associated with failure aside—and evaluate your failure for what it is—the process can be far more defining than success.

Whether we accept it or not, failure often helps us think clearly. It forces us to analyse and plan better.

There is an inherent tendency to reward winning and to shun failure. But even amid such hostility towards failure, there are those who consider failing a gift. That you need to fail to succeed is not really an oxymoron.

Writing this book has been a revelation for me. It forced me to rigorously explore my own feelings about failure. I am your quintessential Indian who wants success but without the pain of failing. The first time I failed in Math, it put me off a subject that had intrigued me. Numbers are fascinating, but it was the fear of failing again that took away that magic of really trying. And that's just one of the many times where I have stepped back for the fear of failure. The agony associated with failing can be overbearing enough to make you walk away.

Reprimanding failure begins very early on in life. From the hobbies we inculcate, to the subjects we choose, to the jobs we opt for—if we think about it—all are intrinsically linked to failure. I know someone who gave up playing the violin to fit in with his peer group. It is this need to 'fit in' that undermines our ability to fail.

But then, even with our cultural conditioning, there are stories of those who have found recipes for success in their failures.

Indian businesses operate in one of the toughest environments in the world. Constant policy flip-flops, loose regulatory framework, and inadequate infrastructure are only some of the challenges; apart from that is the Indian mindset that places too much emphasis on stability and clarity of purpose very early on in life. A society that forces us to fit into boxes—so much so that there is no room to fail.

But then there are the outliers, the visionaries who cannot fit in, and that's how they have gone and built some of the largest corporations in the country which have defined, in more ways than one, India's economic trajectory.

The late Dhirubhai Ambani, founder of India's largest conglomerate, Reliance Industries, built the company at a time when capital costs were so high that most companies would be made unprofitable or failed. But Dhirubhai continued to dream, fail, dream again, until he finally succeeded.

The sixteen failure, aka success, stories chronicled in this book are an attempt to start a conversation on failure, to encourage those reading the book to get out of the box, to pursue their dreams not for love of success but for the adventure of failure, to not let others decide the life you want to live for the fear of failure.

India today is brimming with entrepreneurial energy and new ideas. Private sector is thriving, the middle class is rising, more and more young people are joining the workforce. And interestingly the young are restless enough to not confine themselves to the cocoons of the tried and tested. They are venturing out and charting their own destinies. This book is for all of us who constantly think about 'what might have been'. It is for those corporate guys who believe learning from failure is pretty straightforward—ask people to reflect on what they did wrong and insist on avoiding similar mistakes in the future. It is for all those entrepreneurs who have chosen their path and have embarked on a journey that would be tumultuous, and more so in the Indian context, to say the least.

Heroism is a bi-product of defeat. It's a trait, a quality that is attained by looking at misfortune and striking back. Almost all of the stories chronicled here are a heady mix of misfortune and heroism.

Franklin D. Roosevelt, the former President of the United States, had this overpowering victory drive which took him through the most exhausting national speaking tour ever indulged in by a US presidential candidate; he experienced his misfortune or defeat in the form of infantile paralysis, a locomotive failure which he fought back with a vengeance as he travelled tirelessly. You will find several stories in here where misfortune has also been the biggest inspiration to succeed.

As Confucious said, 'Our greatest glory consists not in never failing, but in rising every time we fall.'

History across the world has been made by extraordinary minds driven by extraordinary failures.

Be cheerful, wipe thine eyes;
Some falls are means the happier to a rise.

William Shakespeare, *Cymbeline*. Act IV, scene ii

It's always better to have tried and failed, than to have not tried at all.

Happy Failing, everyone!

'...the truth is that, in a competition, the weakest part of you comes to the forefront'

ABHINAV BINDRA

Abhinav Bindra made history when he brought India its first individual gold medal in the Olympics in 2008. His relationship with shooting is much like that of an obsessive lover with his muse—stormy, with its highs and lows. There was a point, after winning the gold, when Bindra wanted to quit shooting. The rest, they say, is history. He has been awarded with India's most prestigious civilian award in India, the Padma Bhushan.

Mind is man. The Bhagavad Gita explains the state of the human mind and its impact on the individual most lucidly and aptly. Quite often, we are left stupefied at our inability to perform a particular action at a crucial moment. *What could have possibly gone wrong*, we wonder.

All of us at some point in our lives have been through that point or phase when something fails us at that particular moment of truth. There comes a point when it's no longer about knowledge or skill alone, but finding the perfect equilibrium when it matters the most. Most often it's that elusive balance of the mind and body which propels us towards success or failure.

Before the world can recognize our successes or failures, we as individuals are the key drivers and the best judge of what we think constitutes our success or failure. For a businessman or a businesswoman, success could mean finding the right investor or cracking the perfect marketing strategy or launching a product ahead of competition; for an artist it might be to get that perfect inspiration to express what (s)he wants to say; for a sportsperson it is probably that last stroke, the last strike, that winning shot for the 'gold'.

BIRD'S EYE

The Gita talks about the two distinct sides of the mind: one facing the world of stimuli that reacts to the objects of the world, and the other facing the within that reacts to the stimuli received. The outer mind facing the object is called the objective mind—in Sanskrit it's called the Manas, and the inner mind is called the subjective mind—in Sanskrit, the Buddhi.[1]

The perfect equilibrium, as described in the Gita, is when the objective and subjective aspects of our mind work in unity. And in moments of doubt, the objective mind readily comes under the discipline of the subjective mind. In other words, the perfect state of mind is when Buddhi takes over.

We have all gone through Arjuna's grief at some point in our lives. While we might be trained to just see the eye of the bird, there will be moments of weakness when we will see beyond that, we will be distracted by the glory and the reward that the job or act will bring.

Even though Arjuna was an accepted man of war, when he entered the battlefield against the Kaurava army of hundreds, the tension was palpable in the air, and it presented an insight into Arjuna's state of mind.

He was impatient to start the war; he was ready to show his great courage and his indomitable energy. According to the Gita, the moment, Arjuna took in the sight of the army of the Kauravas, there was a complete shattering of his mental equilibrium. There was a split in his mind, he no longer saw just the eye of the bird, there was an anxious desire in him for a victorious end. His mind was preoccupied with dreaming about the ultimate end of the war which means a complete divorce between the subjective and the objective aspects of his mind.

---

1 Reference: The Holy Geeta: Commentary by Swami Chinmayananda

Let's draw a parallel between Arjuna, the warrior's experience in the battlefield, and ace shooter Abhinav Bindra's performance at the London Olympics in 2012. Bindra's failure to win the gold was directly linked to his mental equilibrium, he says.

WHY I FAILED AT THE LONDON OLYMPICS

Shooting is a sport of immense focus and concentration. Also, like any other sport, or for that matter any other profession, it has its limits on how skilled you can get. After a point, the winner is the one who is able to achieve that perfect equilibrium and just focus on the target at that crucial moment. Focus is far easier written or talked about than practiced. It's a challenge we all fight in our day-to-day lives. To put aside external and internal stimuli or distractions, and to be able to only see your target and be consumed by it, requires persistence, patience, and practice. Bindra was technically as well-prepared for the London Olympics as he could be. 'I was very well-prepared for London. I trained more intensively. I was more informed in London than what I was going into Beijing,' he says.

So what went wrong as he fired the deciding shot that would have taken him to the finals and inched him closer to the elusive gold medal for India?

That Bindra was under tremendous pressure would be a colossal understatement keeping in mind the expectations he was carrying with him, not only of the entire nation, but his own too.

After winning a gold at the Beijing Olympics in 2008, he was expected to win it again. He had done it once. He had played against the best in the world and won a gold at a time when a silver or a bronze at the Olympics was considered a big win for India.

In terms of his mental state, Bindra says, he was technically in a very good frame of mind. He worked towards not letting the 2008 win or the media frenzy around it intimidate him. He did not read newspapers or watch television news for nearly a year. He was single-mindedly focussed on training for the sport. In fact, he says, he was better trained for the London Olympics than he was for Beijing.

However, at the Olympics or any other competition for that matter, you reach your limits on how skilled you can get. 'In my sport, there were 58 participants; 30 could have won on any given day. What differentiates the winner is the person who is able to bring everything together on that particular day in that particular moment.'

And that was Bindra's failure. He couldn't bring all his energies together at that very moment when he fired the deciding shot. He was not as frantic. Not as desperate.

'In London, I was relaxed, composed, and calm. Theoretically it should have worked well. But it doesn't work that way. You have to have rage. You have to be desperate. A part of your mind will be anxious, fearful. Any person would face these emotions. You know tomorrow is the day. To win, you have to have the ability to endure those difficult moments. In London, I was not scared. I was relaxed, normal, happy, calm, and composed. There were parts of me that carried insecurity. I knew I had won the last time and now everyone expected me to win this time. But I did a good job of keeping them aside, by focussing on the moment. But the truth is that, in a competition, the weakest part of you comes to the forefront. You have to be able to endure the moment of weakness. It's painful, it kills you from inside. You have to be resilient enough to endure those feelings.'

Bindra's approach towards that moment of vulnerability was that of an escapist. He had trained his mind so well to not let the external stimuli distract him that he even managed to bury the paranoia to win deep within him. His exterior reflected the state of his mind which was at ease. He wasn't as psyched, paranoid, as he was in Beijing.

'I don't believe in confidence—confidence doesn't help you win. A thought in your mind can change the whole muscle tension in your body. You have to find that perfect state. You start getting confident. You relax—positive thoughts come to you and then your muscle tension weakens. A thought is enough to change the whole dynamics of the body.

'Desire, determination, deep need, a deep hunger is the difference between winning and losing. There is more of a deep desire now than what I had before going to London.

'In Beijing I needed it. In London I wanted it. There is a difference.

'Gagan Narang (Narang won a bronze in Air Rifle Shooting –Men's 10-m Rifle event at the 2012 London Olympics) was desperate. He had missed out in Beijing. He was like I was after Athens. I didn't think there is much difference between his skill and mine. But that's the difference between going a little bit further.'

Abhinav Bindra failed to qualify for the London Olympic finals in 2012.

WHY I WON

In 2008, when Bindra represented India at the Beijing Olympics, theoretically Bindra's mind was in a terrible state for the competition. He was desperate to the point that he had begun to hate the sport he had breathed and lived all his life. Bindra began shooting when he was thirteen.

Beijing happened four years after the Athens Olympics. In 2004 at Athens, Bindra scored 597 in the qualification round and was placed third. The Olympic record was 599.

'In my mind I had a medal in 2004, but I didn't have anything to show for it. I went back with a vengeance (to Beijing in 2008): I wanted to show I could do it. I was desperate.'

Bindra describes the period around the 2004 Athens Olympics as the 'darkest phase' of his career.

'I was so heartbroken that I wanted to leave,' Bindra recalls eight years later.

At Beijing, Bindra was desperate to win. 'More than anyone, I had something to prove to myself, to the world,' he says. He needed the medal with a vengeance. He needed it for his survival.

'In Beijing I was so immersed in my performance that I didn't even realize I had won.' There was no love for the sport, no optimism, no lofty visions of him winning the medal and the accolades that would come with it. There was only frustration and desperation. There was sadness, a deep desire, hunger to win.

'I was in a sad state of mind. I hated my sport. There was a deep desire within my gut, which pushed me. It's this deep desire which helps you in critical moments, where you are about to give up and you don't. It's a minor difference. I have experienced both aspects of it. But that's the difference between winning and losing,' he says talking about his performance at Beijing.

Theoretically, he says, he was in a total mess. His state of mind was far from being what is called as conducive for competition. He was not optimistic or cool-headed—all attributes necessary for a good show. He was paranoid, insecure, tired, and psyched. Yet, he managed to gain that perfect equilibrium of the mind when it mattered the most. He only saw the 'eye of the bird'. In that crucial moment, he was doggedly focussed on his target; at that second, it didn't matter whether he would lose or win. He just had to focus all his energies into getting the most out of that second when he fired the winning shot.

No one was expecting Bindra to bring home a gold. The fact that India was even at the Olympics in the shooting category was a matter of great pride and honour.

While Bindra was not burdened by the expectations of a nation, he wanted to prove to himself that he could win the gold he had been dreaming of winning every single morning since he was sixteen.

Bindra was twenty five when he won the gold for India. He became the first Indian to win an individual gold medal at the Olympic games. It was India's first gold medal since 1980.

At the 2008 Beijing Olympics, Abhinav Bindra brought India perhaps its biggest sporting glory. He outscored all other shooters in the finals. Bindra scored a 10.8 while his closest competitor came with 9.7.

Winning in Beijing meant many things to Abhinav: It was a life-changing experience in many ways; it was proving to himself and the world that he could do it, it was vindication of twelve years of relentless work and practice, it was a dream come true, it was achievement of a goal that perhaps seemed too ambitious for many.

'The night before Beijing I never slept, not even for a moment,' he says.

'At the Olympics, everybody will have a mental failure in my sport. This is a sport of perfection; you cannot afford a mistake; you have to be perfect on an imperfect day. It's a 60-shot competition, and you cannot make a mistake. You are in the sport, you have 20 shots to go, you know you cannot afford a mistake. And the size of the mistake is: you shoot a 9.9, 10 is a bulls eye. As the rules go, you are penalized one full point. To overcome those moments when you get anxious, to find that discipline, when you are having a mentally weak moment, you put your rifle down and start again. Some shots will be easy and some will cost a lot of energy. You have to be able to give everything to overcome that moment.'

After winning a dream he had longed for, breathed, lived,

every single day since he was thirteen, a gut-wrenching void filled Abhinav's life. He had accomplished his dream.

Winning a gold for India had been much more than a passion, it was an obsession for Bindra that defined him, his skill, his sport, his being. The Beijing win left him immensely fulfilled, yet empty. His love and drive for the gold had consumed him to the extent that after he had won it, there was a sense of vacuousness that permeated him.

There was nothing more left in his mind to accomplish in a sport that had been in his life ever since he could remember. Each day, since he was thirteen, had been structured around the sport. Life, as he had known, had been about preparing himself to win the gold. Practice sessions, meditation, training of the mind—all these had filled his days for more than a decade. The eye of the bird was the gold.

And now that he had done it, he says, there was nothing more in the sport to work towards. So much so that Bindra decided to give up shooting after winning the gold in Beijing.

His quest for gold had consumed him to the extent that he had begun to hate the sport for the stresses and pressures it put him through. For Bindra, shooting had ceased to be just a sport, it had morphed into an expression of himself, and he constantly judged himself on his performance. There was a constant pull, which led to tremendous anxiety and pressure and while it propelled him to better his skill, it also filled him with resentment towards the sport.

'The victory had left a big void in my life. For 16 years,

wanting the medal was part of my being. I dreamt that I wanted to win the gold every single night. Every morning I woke up with this goal. After the medal, I was ready, but I had nowhere to go.'

The two years that followed the win were a journey of self-discovery again, of finding a goal, a love, a passion, an aim. Bindra had an aim in life from ever since he could remember and had taken every step, every move to nurture and fulfil that ambition. Every step, every move had been strategically planned. There was nothing left to chance, nothing for contemplation. It was path well travelled, traversed, with postmarks and checkmarks, and no room to miss the goal points.

As a teenager, when most kids were spending most of their time dreaming or wandering aimlessly, Abhinav would spend his days practising in the shooting range, and participating in championship events. Every competition was a step towards winning that gold. It had to happen, it was inevitable, Bindra had not left himself a choice.

He had trained hard, acuminated his skill, had gone through a vigorous training of the mind, and over the years he had nurtured a monstrous need, a gigantic desire to win the medal. He had to do it.

'When I started out, my biggest ambition was to win a club competition, then a district competition. The benchmark kept going up and up. I kept progressing steadily.'

After winning the gold in Beijing, Abhinav gave up shooting and dabbled in business. But running a business could not engage Bindra for long. He constantly felt the need to fill a void, a gaping hole.

He was restless, as if yearning for something. But for what? The sport didn't excite him anymore; in fact the thought of it brought back memories of his days of loathing, when he punished himself with brutal schedules and the need to win.

He says, he was clear in his mind that he didn't want to go back to shooting. After winning the gold in Beijing, he was convinced that he had lost his love for the sport.

What followed were months and months of listlessly hankering for a new life, a new goal, a new ambition, a passion, Abhinav went for a meditative course, called Vipassana, which in Pali language means to see things as they really are.

Vipassana is an ancient meditative technique rediscovered by Gautam Buddha more than 2500 years ago. It is a way of self-transformation through self-observation. It focusses on the deep interconnection between mind and body. It requires disciplined attention to the physical sensations.

'I went through Vipassana to find some direction in life. I went thinking that I wanted to move on. I had done everything. At Vipassana, you meditate, and you don't talk. Those ten days, I realized that my mind could only go back to shooting. And that I really liked shooting.'

It was sometime in around 2010 that Abhinav rekindled his wild romance with the sport he had a love-hate relationship with. He had loved it with an obsession and hated it with a vengeance.

He says—it was start of a fresh journey. Beijing was behind him, his medals and achievements gave him the confidence, but he knew in sports 'yesterday never counts'.

'You win, and the very next day, everybody is looking at what is he going to do next. Every time you do it, it is for the first time, in theory.'

Abhinav also came back with perspective. After spending nearly two decades chasing the gold medal, he says, 'you realize that gold medals are not everything in life. This is one aspect of life. When you do well, you realize that it will not always be like this. You will win some. You will lose some.'

He trained with as much rigour and renewed focus for the London Olympics.

'I was very well-prepared for London. I trained more intensively. But I was not desperate.'

WHY I FAILED
I was not desperate enough to win

Advice

- You cannot be focussed on the outcome. When you are performing, you have to be completely immersed in that moment

- You have to have the ability to cut the thoughts of winning, achievement, medals away from you. The moment you think you can win gold, you will lose focus

*'Neat packages presented
as success don't teach me and the
world anything'*

ANU AGA

Anu Aga has accomplished in a lifetime what most people can only aspire to in many. She led a near 30 billion dollar group, Thermax, from 1996 to 2004. Taking on the reins from her husband, she pushed through difficult decisions, and has been a driving force behind the turnaround of the group. A recipient of the Padma Shri for her work in the field of education, she is also the chairperson of Teach For India foundation and a member of the Rajya Sabha in the Indian Parliament.

Galileo Galilei, the Italian physicist, mathematician, astronomer, and philosopher who played a major role in the scientific revolution, was being rather delphic when he noted, 'Doubt is the father of invention. Plod on, embrace your doubt, and thrive.'

Almost everyone—management gurus, teachers, business leaders, psychiatrists—will emphasize on the mantra 'Believe in Yourself.' Leaders ought to be confident to be able to lead effectively. However, intermittent feelings of self-doubt can turn you into a more humble, motivated, and an awakened leader.

Robert Sutton in his book *Good Boss, Bad Boss* says, 'The best bosses dance on the edge of overconfidence, but a healthy dose of self-doubt and humility saves them from turning arrogant and pigheaded. Bosses who fail to strike this balance are incompetent, dangerous to follow, and downright demeaning.'

Fear of making mistakes can actually raise alertness and intensity. When Anu Aga, director and former chairperson of Thermax Ltd, the 32.46 billion rupee energy and enviornment efficiency business, suddenly found herself at the helm of the company after her husband's sudden death, she went through a period of immense self-doubt. Rohinton Aga was the chairman and managing director and Aga was leading the human resources department.

Finance and technology were never her interest areas; business did not fascinate her, people did. Thermax, an engineering company, set up by her father A.S. Bhathena in 1966 as Wanson (India) to provide engineering solutions, had grown exponentially under her husband's leadership.

The very soft spoken, understated Aga constantly compared herself to her 'very charismatic and dynamic' husband. As she drew comparisons, it dawned on her that she could not be him. But Aga could not celebrate the differences in their personalities, instead they kept reinforcing her feelings of self-doubt. She constantly questioned if she had what it took to lead a company, to successfully run the business her father and husband had built.

It was only love and passion for the company that could overpower her feeling of self-doubt. While business did not pique her interest, her love for the company was unconditional. It was a legacy, an inheritance. She had to get back on her feet and hold on to the reins of the company that had been painstakingly nurtured over years. But how? She was not Rohinton Aga, the man who had so effortlessly gone about making pioneering decisions.

'As a person where I failed was at recognizing my strengths. Men are very brash and talk about their positives and strengths. Women are full of self-doubt. Especially since it was a family-owned business, I kept asking myself, have I been chosen because I own 62 percent of the shares or because I am the right person to head my company? I was devaluing myself all the time. And I think when you devalue yourself, you have to have a realistic appraisal of both your strengths and weaknesses, and not focus on your weaknesses alone. I also kept comparing myself to my husband—which is not a nice thing to do. An apple can never give you orange juice. And if I only want orange juice, I won't even enjoy the apples. I can never be my husband. My skill sets are different.'

To cope with the grief of losing her husband, and subsequently her son, and to come to terms with the new set of responsibilities, Anu Aga went through ten intensive days of Vipassana, the Buddhist discipline of meditation.

'Vipassana helped me come to terms with my husband's death. It was there that I realized that I could never be my husband, and that I have the option to take help from others. I asked myself: what is stopping me from taking help from others?'

Soon after Aga took charge at Thermax as its chairperson, India would go through an economic downturn in the late nineties. The company had just gone public (listed on the stock exchange) in 1995, but Aga says, 'We were still operating in a private company mindset.'

Anu Aga's husband, Rohinton Aga, had diversified into several businesses. 'He was a real visionary and had several wonderful ideas,' she says. But she also realized that perhaps some of those ideas were ahead of their time, such as getting into the wind energy business.

The company got into wind energy at a time when there were no tax breaks for wind energy companies.

'Many such businesses added to our topline, but eroded our bottomline. When I took over, though I was not a business person, I had basic common sense and intuition. I knew we couldn't continue businesses that were not adding to our profits.'

Gradually, Aga regained confidence in her abilities to run the business, and took tough decisions that are usually hardest to take. She realized the company was in denial and had settled to 'satisfactory under performance'. There was an economic slowdown to justify the shrinking bottomline.

Most often, the best of us, will find the most legitimate excuses for a slackening performance. We tend to internalize our reasons or excuses to the degree that we believe in them more than in our own abilities.

'All my executives, who were men, kept saying, "Don't worry, we will come up again. There is no need for any changes." They kept saying that the person most affected was me, since I was the majority shareholder.'

It was after Aga received an anonymous letter from an unhappy shareholder that she truly comprehended the quantum of responsibility that lay on her. Contrary to what she had been told about the poor performance affecting primarily her and her family—the majority shareholders— she realized that 40 percent owners of the company were the shareholders who had placed their faith in Thermax. The shareholder blamed Anu Aga for her inaction. It was that letter that convinced her that the company needed an outside perspective.

'We were showing profits on our balance sheet, because we had just gone public. I realized we were making an operational loss, and we just had a good balance sheet because of our treasury income.'

Anu Aga was brutally honest and brave as she announced the state of the company in a press meet; she was forthright that the company was slipping and highlighted the need for urgent action.

'Everyone said that you don't expose your company like

that. Thank God I did it. Because if you are not in tune with the problem, how will you fix it? It showed me in very bad light. But to me if your foundation is not solid, and you don't admit it, it will remain shaky. You have got to look at the reality. You have to differentiate between being and doing.'

When Aga thought of bringing in a consultant to do a stock check, she faced resistance from almost everyone in the company. Colleagues and employees questioned her and were fairly adamant in their opposition.

'When I wanted to engage a consulting company to help us, all senior executives advised against them. "We have never followed their advice," they said. But I was very firm; I brought it to the board and convinced them. Men find it very difficult to ask for help. It goes against their macho image.'

Yet again, Anu Aga had come to terms with her failure and taken corrective steps to address it. Even as she had veiled herself under a cloud of self-doubt, she managed to retain her ability to step back and analyze the situation, and even herself, from an outsider's perspective.

'I always felt I will not compromise when I don't want to. I make mistakes. I have the courage of conviction. The more you do things you believe in, it strengthens you and your belief in yourself.'

She hired the services of Boston Consulting Group (BCG). What followed were a series of tough decisions—Aga further streamlined the business, Thermax exited some of the non-core verticals, and introduced a performance-based culture. All decisions required Anu Aga to be firm, resolute, determined, and sure.

'You cannot learn or address failure without acknowledging it. You cannot think you are an ostrich . You have to take very strong and definitive steps to correct a problem.'

'We had always thought the purpose of business is also to generate employment. My husband and I had thought that even with a few non-performers we could carry on as long as they were honest. But in a competitive market, I realized we cannot. Employee cost is about 17-18 percent. We brought in an incentive system and we reconstituted the entire board.'

Earlier, Thermax would acknowledge good work done by an employee by promoting them to the board. When Anu Aga took over, the board had nine executive directors.

'But when things went wrong, the same executives couldn't evaluate their own work objectively. They were always coming up with excuses. I realized we had to change. BCG helped me think very differently.'

The board was reconstituted to bring in more independent directors. The turnaround focussed on divesting non-core businesses. The company restructured into six core businesses in energy and environment. Operational efficiency brought down employee cost from 16 percent of the turnover to less than 7.5 percent. The promoter members stepped down from executive positions and operational aspects were left to non-family members—a professional team led by the managing director.

'Because if you are not in tune with the problem, how will you fix it? It showed me in a bad light—after I took over after my husband's death, the company went into losses. And that was the reality.'

But Anu Aga never fused her 'being' with her 'doing'. She did not let her doing define her being.

'You have to differentiate between being and doing. I have to give a lot of affection to my being. But I am also doing and it cannot be without failures. Spontaneous doing has to go through failures. It is up to each person to determine how to treat his or her doing. However, one has to respect one's being. This is unconditional. The whole phenomenon of failure is the law of nature.'

'Neat packages presented as success don't teach me and the world anything. But sharing my vulnerability teaches a lot.'

WHY I FAILED

- I tried to be someone else
- I tried to capitalize on strengths I did not have and ignored what I did

Advice

- Never confuse your being with your doing

- Strengths and weakness are a part of a human being. Apply all your strengths to your work

- Rely on your intuition

- Have faith in your common sense

- Remember, you don't have to live the way the world expects you to. Do things which give you satisfaction

*'My obituary was written in 1999...
this life now is all a bonus'*

MADHUR BHANDARKAR

Madhur Bhandarkar is a filmmaker with a difference. His cinema is unlike the grandeur and mush of Bollywood. With his first hit film, *Chandni Bar*, he told the story of the bar girls in Mumbai. What has followed since are a series of films reflecting on the different aspects of the society we live in. Films like *Corporate* and *Page 3* were dubbed as a disturbingly accurate portrayal of our society. Known for his thorough research and eye for detail, he says, if he weren't a director, he would have been a journalist.

'I made my first film the way everyone wanted me to; with *Chandni Bar* I went with my own gut, conviction, and instinct.'

Failure, much like success in the entertainment universe, takes on gargantuan dimensions. You are a star one day, and a nobody the next. And there is really no one who wants to know, be around, or even be associated with a nobody. The severity of such extreme reactions is magnified manifold in the world of films. Madhur Bhandarkar's journey in the film world is teeming with failure, rejection, tears, and humiliation. And this cycle of rejection and failure, he says, continued for decades until he made his first hit film *Chandni Bar* that catapulted his status overnight from a nobody to a somebody.

It has been an overwhelming, unbelievable, awe-inspiring life fraught with setbacks, challenges, failures, and lessons. Bhandarkar grew up in an India where education was considered the only way out of an existence of mediocrity and drudgery of middle-class households. His father, an electrical contractor, couldn't have financially supported his education for too long, and Bhandarkar realized that fairly early on in life.

THE BATTLE BETWEEN DESIRE AND RESPONSIBILITY

He would have been thirteen or fourteen when he failed his class sixth exams and decided to give up studying further. He knew his family would not be able to pay for the extra tuition he required and so instead he decided to become a video cassette delivery boy. 'I didn't know what to do. I knew

I had to do something. Things were so bad that even the ten rupees I would bring home would make a difference in the way we lived.'

Bhandarkar delivered video cassettes for nearly five years, a job that fuelled his passion for films. 'I watched films all the time. When children my age were reading *Chandamama* (a children's magazine), I would read titles of movies.'

His first and only education was through films and books. An avid reader, Bhandarkar would try and read whatever came his way—that's how he says he learnt English and was one of the very few video cassette delivery boys in the city of Mumbai who could and would converse in English with the customers. 'I am flamboyant and I am a good observer of people, and that's what has been reflected in my films.'

When Bhandarkar decided to become a filmmaker, he was rightfully apprehensive about sharing his ambition with the family that was counting on him to make their lives better. The only son who was expected to go to Muscat, earn money through small but better paying jobs, and pull the family through. The son of an electric contractor could not possibly join an industry that had been a jamboree of the privileged, moneyed, and connected.

'My mother wanted me to go to Muscat and get a job there. I didn't know what to do. There was an overwhelming sense of responsibility towards them and then there was this deep desire in me to make films.'

Bhandarkar worked on the sets of several filmmakers, picking up shoes, sweeping the floor on a conveyance allowance of thirty rupees—a part of which he would try and save by walking to studios and skipping meals—before he finally took the plunge into filmmaking.

WHEN YOU DON'T LISTEN TO YOUR HEART

The luxury to let Bhandarkar scrimp through with thirty rupees a day to follow his dreams was not what his family could afford; the necessity to earn was dire and the sense of responsibility towards family overwhelming. Bhandarkar made an attempt to achieve what his family had always aspired for—a near-ordinary life, with basic amenities and enough money to not worry where the next meal would come from. Bhandarkar's search for a life away from the everyday battles of survival took him to Muscat and Dubai, but he says, 'I got bored there and decided to come back.'

Bhandarkar could not get himself to work in the warehouses and factories. So against all the odds stacked against him, including the humiliation and emotional turmoil of not being able to live up to any expectations, he listened to that bray of the heart and decided to come back to Mumbai. Homecoming was hostile to say the least. But Bhandarkar had never expected it to be easy, and perhaps that gave him the conviction to block out the noise and follow what was an elusive dream.

WHEN YOU FAIL YOUR FIRST REAL CHANCE

'I would wake up in the morning not knowing where to go.'

Bhandarkar remained in this state of listlessness for months, until he met film director Ram Gopal Verma and assisted him in the making of *Rangeela*. After working as an assistant director in four of Verma's films, Bhandarkar found the courage and confidence to direct his own film. 'But without a hero, or any star support, nobody would back me.'

After trying for nearly two years, Bhandarkar found support in a Mumbai-based film conglomerate—Bombino. A large organization's support meant that Bhandarkar had little or no room to negotiate what he wanted in the film. 'Bombino gave me an opportunity but wanted a commercial film. I told myself beggars can't be choosers. I had no choice.'

Bhandarkar's first film, *Trishakti*, took three years to make. It was a film where Bhandarkar was led more by the commercial viability of the film than his own intuition and instincts.

'There were no reviews of the film. On the Friday of the film release, I had gone to a friend's place, who didn't know that my film had released that day. I just broke down that night. The film had bombed. I thought my career was over. Nobody wanted to associate with me. Everyone told me it was over for me and I should go back to Ram Gopal Verma. My parents told me to go back to Muscat. There was negativity everywhere. I was nearly thirty with nothing to show. My obituary was written.'

What followed was another year of struggle. Bhandarkar would borrow hundred rupees to travel around the city in buses to meet producers. Whatever little brand equity Bhandarkar had built over a decade was destroyed overnight, and with that Bhandarkar lost out on all the 'friends' in the industry.

'People would ignore me blatantly. They would walk away, not respond to phone calls. I was not invited anywhere. This phase was a huge learning experience. I was boycotted by almost everyone.'

Bhadarkar's routine was to traverse the city on buses and spend time on a phone booth with fifty to sixty coins to make calls to almost everyone he thought could help.

A year went by, Bhandarkar had made no progress. In fact, his reputation had taken a beating and his credibility as a filmmaker was scarred, and he didn't have the connections or the money to fight back.

WHEN THE VOLCANO ERUPTED

Bhandarkar persisted in his journey, and it was during one of those long, dark nights that he found himself at a dance bar in Mahim in Mumbai, strangely intrigued by the sadness and irony behind the dim lights, brightly coloured faces, and the blaring loud music.

'I was aghast to see the dancing girls. I came from a very middle-class family and for me to be sitting in a dance bar was very embarrassing at a level. I was apprehensive. I didn't want to be spotted by anyone. For me, that would have been one more negative thing against Madhur Bhandarkar. I sat there for thirty minutes, but after I came back home, what I had seen at the bar kept hounding me.'

And there began the journey towards what would later culminate into an award-winning film, *Chandni Bar*.

After that experience, Bhandarkar would go to a dance bar almost every night. Sometimes four or five different kinds in a night—from the elite to the cheap, dingy bars. This was part of Bhandarkar's research for the film that was still taking form and shape in his mind. He moved from the sitting area to the make-up rooms of almost 60 dance bars in Mumbai, where slowly he says, 'The girls started opening up and sharing their life stories with me.'

Bhandarkar knew the film he wanted to direct, but the challenge lay in finding a producer. He met nearly fifteen producers who dismissed the idea and the film. They were convinced that a stark, dark film on the life of a woman from a dance bar would not work commercially. A slew of rejections did not shake Bhandarkar's conviction in his idea of the film.

'I knew that this time I wanted to make the film the way I wanted to. I went with my gut, feel, and conviction. In my first film I wasn't sure. I made the film the way everyone wanted me to. I had thought to myself that I will make this film the way I want to.'

Bhandarkar found a supporter in R. Mohan, who was ready to produce the film, but now the challenge was to get the lead actor to agree. Bhandarkar had written the film with Tabu as the lead. She was a reining star in the year 2000, when Bhandarkar started work on the film.

The challenge was to get her to agree to work with a rookie director whose first film had sunk without a whimper.

'I was under tremendous pressure while narrating the script to Tabu. When I reached the interval, she said, "Stop. I can imagine myself in the character." It was as if a volcano erupted inside me.'

Bhandarkar made the film exactly the way he wanted to. He went with his gut feel, thought, and conviction. Before the release of the film, Bhandarkar staved off the negativity from other filmmakers who would often comment on the title of the film. It had been almost three years since his first flop, and expectations from Bhandarkar were low.

'During the special screening of the film, I was in the hall and nobody even gave me a second look. During the interval, nobody reacted to the film. I was nervous and apprehensive. But when the film ended, the entire hall gave me a standing ovation and I was just stunned!'

Bhandarkar, who till then had been a flop filmmaker, a nobody, had transformed in those few hours into one of the brightest directors in Bollywood. 'In those three hours the entire equation changed. People couldn't believe that the same Madhur Bhandarkar who had made *Trishakti* had also made *Chandni Bar*.'

'People who wouldn't look at me earlier, started calling me up. I became the blue-eyed boy of the industry.'

'If *Trishakti* wouldn't have flopped, I would have stuck to the same pattern and fizzled out very quickly. I realized that neither success nor failure is permanent. When I got the National Award, I had to pinch myself.'

WHY I FAILED

- I didn't follow my intuition
- I let people dictate what they wanted me to be

Advice

- Don't let circumstances faze you

- Do what you love. It's better to be the king of hell, than a slave in heaven

'I had learnt that professionals should not get influenced by political influences. 1982-83 was the heyday of political interference in banks, but for me it was a shocker.'

NARAYANAN VAGHUL

Narayanan Vaghul, banker, Padma Bhushan, one of the financial architects of India. He has been a key driving force behind the transformation of ICICI from a development financial institution to India's second largest bank. It's been his foresight and vision that has given wings to many dreams. A visionary, he is known to understand ideas and concepts that most don't. Former chairman of ICICI bank, he is a visiting professor at The Stern School of Business. He also serves as director on the board of several companies.

FAILING BY DESIGN

Designing or strategizing your failure could propel you to be a catalyst in driving greater change, attaining a higher purpose, and striving for excellence.

When King Ashoka, the third monarch of the Indian Mauryan Dynasty, won the battle of Kalinga, one of the bloodiest battles in world history, he viewed his success as a regrettable failure which ultimately propelled him towards Buddhism. Later, Buddhism would become the most influential force in Ashoka's life, and became a catalyst for the beginning of a peaceful and most glorious chapter of his reign. 'Amidst the tens of thousands of names of monarchs that crowd the columns of history...the name of Asoka shines, and shines almost alone, a star,' is what British historian H.G. Wells wrote on Ashoka.

While Ashoka won the battle of Kalinga, he designed his failure, which led him to ultimately attain a higher purpose. The death and destruction, the bloodshed, the sense of failing his people prodded him to unleash reforms that would later bring him the title of Ashoka the Great.

Failure by design has been adopted by several bright, extraordinary minds for various reasons. Narayanan Vaghul, a foremost financial visionary, a key driving force behind building a financial institution in India that continues to be pioneering in many ways, too designed his own failure when he resigned from the position of chairman of Bank of India—a position that wields great power and authority. Vaghul was appointed as chairman in 1981. Eighties was a decade that many refer to as one of the darkest hours of India.

Growth was painfully slow, entrepreneurship was marred by strict controls, and insecure political leadership at the Centre only added to the uncertainty. It was Indira's India which was politically tumultuous, economically poor (India in the eighties grew at 3.5 percent) and excessively socialist.

Barring a few, almost every industry was under strict government control, including banking. And as chairman, Vaghul had a daunting job of exercising independence in decision making in a public sector bank at a time when government interference in private and public sector was rampant.

Being chairman of a bank was one of the most sought after positions for the power it brought with it. 'I was only forty four years of age, it was supposed to be a coup for a person like me to be appointed as the chairman of the Bank of India. Everybody expected me to continue as the chairman for the next sixteen years,' says Vaghul. He was the youngest chairman of a public sector bank in India.

But N. Vaghul says he failed at striking that elusive balance between exercising autonomy with political interference. There were expectations beyond the purview of his professional capacity to manage, orders to take, and compromises to be made. Vaghul had to work with a myriad set of people and their political motivations.

The bank was a government-owned entity and Vaghul's principles did not allow him to take crucial decisions at the behest of political entities. Vaghul had the commitment, the vision, and the ideas to make the bank grow. But the political interference in the running of the bank disappointed him and he decided to quit. He failed at balancing his expectations of himself and of others. He was dispirited to the extent that he allowed his motivation and drive to be eclipsed by external influences.

'Looking back, I don't think I was in a position to take on the challenge of political influence over Bank of India,' he laments.

As Vaghul resigned from a coveted position of power, he might have been considered a failure by many, but for Vaghul, he had truly succeeded as a professional.

Most often, failures of businesses, as of individuals, are attributed to the inability to take tough decisions at the right time. To quit might have been a tough decision for Vaghul, but he knew the time was right and his reasons were beyond compromise.

'I had learnt that professionals should not get influenced by political influences. 1982-83 was the heyday of political interference in banks, but for me it was a shocker.'

Before Vaghul was appointed as chairman of Bank of India, he was working with the Central Bank of India. Since he was not heading the bank, he was oblivious to the political pressures and challenges that came with it.

CALLING IT QUITS

In 1983, Vaghul decided to quit banking. 'At the age of forty seven, I called it a day,' and retired to Chennai. At an age when most professionals are reaching the peak of their careers, Vaghul opted for a semi-retired life. It was an unconventional, bold decision. To move on from the centre of power to a life of oblivion was definitely not the norm. But for Vaghul, the decision was inevitable.

He recalls a conversation with the then Reserve Bank of India Governor, the current Prime Minister, Manmohan Singh: 'I told him: There are two kinds of people who can be chairman—those who are hankering for power and those who are hankering for money. I am neither.'

'A man with limited ambition' is how Vaghul describes himself. With two lakh rupees in his savings, he relocated to Chennai with his wife. He started again, from a modest two bedroom apartment, away from the banking world, as a writer with the *Hindu*.

'I had never written before; the writing job made me Rs 3,000 a month, and that was my income.'

Vaghul's passion for ideas, entrepreneurship, and finance brought him back to banking. The new Prime Minister in office—the young, dynamic Rajiv Gandhi who had been chosen after the assassination of Indira Gandhi—gave him confidence that political pressures could be resisted politely and firmly.

'Rajiv Gandhi brought a breath of fresh air,' he says.

Vaghul was almost touching fifty when he embarked on a defining phase of his career that would stamp him as a visionary, an ideas man, a reformist.

In 1985, Vaghul was appointed as chairman of the then Industrial Credit and Investment Corporation of India (ICICI), now known as ICICI Bank. Vaghul led the transformation of ICICI from a small size, long-term credit bank to India's second largest bank.

Vaghul understood ideas that seemed ahead of their time to many. He disbursed loans for small businesses, he betted on nascent concepts that would later grow into conglomerates and play an instrumental role in putting India on the global map. Biocon, India's largest biotechnology company, was one such company which got its initial round of funding from ICICI. Vaghul showed confidence in Biocon when its founder, Kiran Mazumdar-Shaw, had been rejected by several banks.

He started India's first venture capital company (ICICI Venture) in 1987, pioneered the concept of credit rating in India by establishing CRISIL, and laid the foundation for a universal banking model which caters to the banking needs of various customer segments. He received the Padma Bhushan from the President of India for his contribution to Indian trade and industry.

Knowing when to walk away is probably one of the tougher decisions in the life of a professional, a politician, or an entrepreneur. As you take that decision, you should know your reasons for doing so—whether to reinvent yourself or to fight for your principle or to find purpose. Often this is the time for introspection, self-evaluation, and great learning.

Vaghul spent twenty-five years with ICICI. He built an institution, brought in the best people, and charted a vision for the organization. The path wasn't easy—besides the operational challenges, Vaghul faced political pressures from the highest political echelons. But this time, Vaghul had come back stronger and determined.

'In ICICI, I felt the same pressures, but I had decided not to give up,' he says.

There were 'threats' and calls from the Prime Minister of India pressurizing Vaghul to take certain decisions that Vaghul didn't approve of.

'I had never seen more blunt talk,' he says, recalling the pulls and pressures he faced building ICICI.

Vagul remembers an instance when a certain minister wanted favours from him in the form of approvals and sanctions that Vaghul didn't agree with. As Vaghul protested, he was threatened with 'serious consequences', including jail. But Vaghul was adamant that neither will he compromise nor quit. Being a firm believer in doing things that he thinks are right, he successfully and firmly resisted the pressure.

'I told him I will not do it.'

It was conviction in himself, in his beliefs and vision, that gave him the courage and confidence to constantly push back.

There were times when Vaghul was literally pushed into a corner. There was no one he could turn to for redressal. It was a battle he had to fight alone.

Vaghul recalls that when he brought up his conversation with the minister who was pushing Vaghul for favours with none other than the Prime Minister. It was the Prime Minister who, after hearing out Vaghul, suggested 'but can't you do this?'

It was a challenging moment for Vaghul, but he did not give in—as he politely and firmly repeated what he had told the minister earlier that he 'could not do it'.

After that conversation, Vaghul didn't hear back from either the Prime Minister or the minister regarding the matter.

When it comes to ethics or principles, there are no compromises for Vaghul. He is currently on the board of organizations like Mahindra & Mahindra, Arcelor Mittal, Wipro Limited, apart from advising several business leaders, entrepreneurs, and growth companies.

WHY I FAILED

- I couldn't balance between my expectations of me and of others
- I couldn't manage the political pressures that came with the position of authority

Advice

- When in doubt, step back and reassess your priorities

- Remember, you don't have to follow others

- Make yourself of steel

- While money is important, aiming on a broader social objective will help you perform better.

- Don't lose sight of your long-term goals

- Never compromise on ethics

'There are two kinds of failures:
perceived and real'

KIRAN MAZUMDAR-SHAW

Kiran Mazumdar-Shaw, shines like an outlier in corporate India. Founder of India's first and largest biotechnology company, Biocon Ltd, Kiran has been a trailblazer as she has gone about charting her destiny and building a billion dollar group. She is a recipient of the prestigious Padma Bhushan and Padma Shri. Mazumdar-Shaw continues to inspire men and women to step out of their comfort zones and break the boundary walls.

'Forget conventionalisms; forget what the world thinks of you stepping out of your place; think your best thoughts, speak your best words, work your best works, looking to your own conscience for approval. I had rather make history than write it. Failure is impossible.' This indubitable advice came from Susan Anthony, a prominent civil rights leader during the women suffrage movement of the 1800s. As cherished the advice is, adopting it has proven to be challenging for women across the world.

Even today, in the 21st century, Anthony's words hold resonance. There are several reasons why women hold themselves back from being the very best they can be—most often allowing culture and society to define their boundaries.

As women go about culturally conditioning themselves to hold back, they also set themselves up for failure. Failure in this context takes on a different meaning.

Women fail themselves when they opt for an 'easier' option than their passion. Or when they go out of their way to fit into the mould. The tendency to refrain or give up even before really trying reflects in the choices women make and that impacts the life they aspire for.

But as Susan Anthony rightly said, history is made by those who look towards their own conscience for approval. And that's what Kiran Mazumdar-Shaw did.

Founder of India's first and largest biotechnology company, she defied conventions as she went about thinking her best thoughts and working her best works. She only sought approval from her own conscience. Mazumdar-Shaw embarked on her entrepreneurial journey when there were hardly any women entrepreneurs in India. Even the entrepreneurs who were women, were often supported by their husbands or family, and Mazumdar-Shaw was one of the few who had set out on her own. She made every effort to stay out of the box and that's how she made history in corporate India.

Interestingly, with every choice she made, she set herself up for failure. She trained as a brewmaster, and failed to find a job. For a woman to be a brewmaster in India at the time was near impossible—she was the first.

It was the India of the seventies, the era of bell bottoms, polyester shirts, and limited imagination. It was the decade which saw India's socialist policies come to the fore as banks were nationalized and royal privy purses abolished. There were really three professions to speak of—medicine, engineering, and finance. All three primarily dominated by men. Entrepreneurship was suffocated with overbearing controls, and again was largely a male domain. It was a time when most women, following convention, married young and chose to become homemakers.

'Almost all my friends were either married or getting married,' said Mazumdar-Shaw. She, however, relentlessly and tirelessly looked for a job as a brewmaster in Bangalore (now, Bengaluru), but couldn't convince anyone to hire her. She tried to fight gender biases as she went from one company to another, answering questions not to prove her ability but to explain her choice of profession—'How could a woman be a brewmaster?' they would ask.

It was because no one wanted to hire a woman as a brewmaster that India's largest biotechnology company, Biocon, was born in a garage of a rented house in Bangalore. Not finding a job was her first failure, which, contrary to being a belittling experience, defined her life in many ways. She was passionate, aware of her strengths, ambitious and courageous. She did not get rejected to give up, but to fight back. What she did not do when she failed to get a job as a brewmaster was to feel defeated. She did not question her own abilities; she instead followed her passion of working with enzymes and used her knowledge to create her own opportunity.

'You must be able to distinguish between a real failure and a perceived one that will help you decide your strategy,' she says.

Such an insightful, analytical approach towards failure could only come from someone who has had the courage to fail, bounce back, and fail again.

Mazumdar-Shaw's choice of working with enzymes and walking down the entrepreneurial path has been fraught with daunting challenges. And with each setback, she has emerged much stronger. Mazumdar-Shaw has featured on *Forbes* Asia's 50 Power Businesswomen lists. She has been awarded the Padma Shri and the Padma Bhushan from the Government of India.

How did she do it? She showed enormous strength, courage, perseverance, and belief in herself and with every failure, she reminded herself that quitting would never be an option for her. She always shook off the ennui and moved ahead.

Failure Is Not Final, Giving Up Is

Daughter of a brewmaster and without a job, raising funds for her entrepreneurial venture was not going to be easy. Mazumdar-Shaw was prepared to fight it out—she knew she would have to stave off opposition at every step.

Mazumdar-Shaw was trying to build an enterprise in an area that was relatively nascent in India, and the fact that she was a woman and had no family money to fall back on didn't help either. She was twenty five at the time.

Getting banks to fund her venture was nearly impossible. Banks wanted her father to be a guarantor. And Kiran disagreed on principle. Being a woman entrepreneur also put her at a disadvantage. But the challenges and setbacks did not hold her back from setting up office with a seed capital of ten thousand rupees—around four lakh rupees today.

'There are many examples of failure. I had a huge credibility hurdle to overcome. I failed to get financial support. I failed to recruit people I wanted to. The first fifteen years were all about survival,' says Mazumdar-Shaw looking back at the initial years of her entrepreneurial life.

Biocon Limited was launched in 1978, in partnership with an Irish Biotechnology company Biocon Biochemicals founded by a first generation Irish entrepreneur Leslie Auchincloss. The company produced enzymes for alcoholic beverages, paper, and other products. Growth was slow, as a pioneer Mazumdar-Shaw faced resistance and discrimination from all quarters—employees didn't want to work for a woman and investors remained wary of investing in a woman-run company.

But Mazumdar-Shaw persevered. The company started to make profits and almost a decade later, Auchincloss sold his stake in Biocon to Unilever.

Though the challenges of her journey would seem insurmountable to many, Shaw went about slicing her setbacks with almost clinical precision. She says, 'You must understand why you are failing. You are failing because your credibility is at stake. You have got to make credibility to ensure people trust you.'

As Mazumdar-Shaw went about building credibility and the company started adding to its bottomline, she also started dreaming bigger. She had understood the scale of her potential and ambition. She wanted to build a global scale company and for that she would have to go beyond enzymes. The focus of the business was changed from enzymes to biopharmaceuticals in the nineties. She sold off the enzyme business she had spent fifteen years building, and put in all her energies into the biopharmaceutical business—where the first batch of enzymes failed.

'Here I was trying to scale up a home grown biotechnology firm and my first batch failed. We checked why it failed. We identified process failures,' she says.

Mazumdar-Shaw took the failure in her stride and did not internalize it, a personality trait most women are guilty of.

Years later, Mazumdar-Shaw failed again, this time at her dream project of building oral insulin. The drug failed to give the desired outcome in the clinical study. It brought down the glucose levels to desired levels, but failed to lower the haemoglobin count in patients with type 2 diabetes to the desired levels. This came out in the late stage clinical trials.

'That was a dark hour. I had built the drug with great expectations,' she laments.

The oral insulin drug was again a pioneering effort by an Indian biopharmaceutical company. There was hype, awe, and immense expectations around it.

But the mountain of expectations did not dwarf Mazumdar-Shaw's spirit. Once again, she analysed what went wrong and how they could do better.

A thorough analysis showed a flaw in the design of the study. 'Let's be pragmatic about failure,' she said. 'If we want to give up this programme, we should. One should be prepared to give up.'

Mazumdar-Shaw had earlier sold off the business that she had spent fifteen years building. 'When I sold my enzyme business, I had given it whatever I could, and I unlocked very good value.'

Mazumdar-Shaw was ready to walk away again. In the oral insulin failure, analysis showed that the design of the clinical trial was wrong. The product was effective but the study results did not meet expectations due to the flaw in the design of the study. Biocon decided to continue the programme with a different study design.

Nearly a year later, in March 2012, Mazumdar-Shaw suffered another setback. Biocon's global partner, Pfizer, and Biocon decided to part ways.

A much talked about deal where Biocon was to develop and produce biosimilar versions of insulin and Pfizer was to commercialize the products in global markets, was called off rather abruptly.

Minutes after the announcement of the break-up, Mazumdar-Shaw was quoted as saying, 'Biocon remains committed to delivering its Biosimilar Insulins portfolio to global markets in its endeavour to make a difference to diabetic patients across emerging and developed economies. Biocon will continue to work with its existing partners in several markets and will pursue a commercial strategy on its own and through new alliances in other markets.'

Mazumdar-Shaw categorizes the Pfizer fallout as a perceived failure. For Mazumdar-Shaw, calling the deal off was the only logical way forward, but for the analysts and media it was a failure. Mazumdar-Shaw had failed to take the much talked about partnership forward. 'Pfizer wanted us to renegotiate the deal. I was not willing to. It was early enough for us to part ways,' she says rather matter-of-factly.

There was a change in Pfizer's business strategy and Biocon didn't agree with it. Mazumdar-Shaw did not wait around for the cynics to settle down, in less than a year, Biocon entered into an agreement with Mylan in February 2013 for co-development and marketing of its biosimilar insulin analog products.

'We were anyways to develop most of the programmes.' I said: 'Let's do it ourselves. I am sure there are other ways to commercialize the product.'

WHY I FAILED

- In my initial years, I couldn't get others to see my vision
- I failed at getting the best talent to work for me during my early years of entrepreneurship
- Pfizer deal fall-out was a perceived failure. We were not looking in the same direction

Advice

- Always distinguish between perceived and real failure
- Break down failure and strategize
- Don't take failure personally
- Whenever you fail, do not have a knee-jerk reaction
- Deal with failure: There is learning in every step

'The optimism got me into trouble and out of trouble'

GORUR RAMASWAMY
IYENGAR GOPINATH
(CAPTAIN GOPINATH)

Captain Gopinath gave the Indian middle class wings with India's first budget airline—Air Deccan. He is known as much for his success and vision, as his failure. A retired Captain of the Indian Army, Captain Gopinath has been a serial entrepreneur, an author, and a politician. His is a story of relentless energy, passion, and adventure.

Can we Learn to Fly?

Perhaps not. We are speaking figuratively of course. You don't need to be a certain personality type to be able to fly or to let your ideas and imagination soar. What you do need is conviction, passion, and courage to chase, persist, and make your dreams happen despite the imperfections. Let's look at the bumblebee, for instance.

It is technically impossible for a bumblebee to fly. According to a report published by Dr Richard Bomphrey of Oxford University, 'Experiments in Fluids', the bumblebee's flight is surprisingly inefficient—aerodynamically-speaking—it's as if the insect is 'split in half' as not only do its left and right wings flap independently but the airflow around them never joins up to help it slip through the air more easily. Bomphrey uses biomechanics to investigate evolutionary biology. But the bumblebee soars. There have been theories that the bumblebee's wings are too small to create sufficient lift. Yet the bumblebee continues to surprise. (S)he defies expectations. Nature never meant for the bumblebee to fly and yet it does.

Yes, we Can

Yes, we have heard it before, and we have heard it often. Not just from the US President Barack Obama, who won elections because he could convince millions of Americans, who were battling insecurities at various levels, that they could accomplish what they wanted, that they could reclaim their life. It is ironical then that it was a message that reaffirmed people of their own abilities helped win Obama a resounding victory. At a level it also goes on to show human psychology that is constantly seeking affirmations from internal as well as external stimuli. Don't we all tend to gravitate towards a life that is expected of us? Or, better, we tend to build a life as others think should be for us. The internal stimuli or our very basic nature is easier to ignore and most often it is the external stimuli that we react to. The human mind is in such a constant paradox that we often let others tell us of our limitations and we consequently let our shortcomings decide the life we should not want to lead. Let me give you an example. Isn't it just easier to accept that I don't understand music enough to make good music, than to consider the possibility that perhaps those giving me feedback have a specific taste and that maybe my genre of music is different and could be an acquired taste. Or, let's go down to an even more basic level. How many times have we let our bosses, teachers, editors tells us that a particular job or a subject or an assignment is not for us, and how many times have we challenged that belief?

It is always easier to succumb. I remember my teacher telling me that Maths was not a subject for me. I, or for that matter my family, never questioned the teacher's ability to make the subject interesting. I was nudged from all sides (family and teachers) to just suffer the subject and then drop it. I was taught to loath it and not love it. It was only much, much later in life that I realized I did find the subject enormously interesting. If only I had not let others decide my shortcomings.

In entrepreneurship too, you will come across naysayers and everything will most likely work against you, especially if you are embarking on the journey with little or no funds. That's when your true belief in your idea will be tested. And it will be entirely on you to keep the fire burning or to let it die.

Captain Gopinath's story of embarking on entrepreneurship after retiring from the army is one such story of immense conviction, a vision, huge success and a heart-breaking failure.

THE BUMBLEBEE PHENOMENON

It was Captain Gopinath who told me about the bumblebee and its determination to fly despite all odds stacked against it—the most formidable one being its basic design or DNA is not conducive to flying. Capt. Gopinath cites the example to explain his tryst with entrepreneurship. An ex-army captain with no money cannot start an airline. But just as the bumblebee with its imperfections chooses to fly, Capt. Gopinath chose to soar despite his reality. He had fought the 1971 Bangladesh Liberation War, and after quitting the army he decided to become a farmer.

'When I left the army, I had Rs 6,000 and I decided to set up a farm with that money. I was so much in love with the notion of living on the land. I had romanticized it. The notion to live on the land and work on it was overpowering. There was no logical analysis on how I was to live, earn money. There was this inextinguishable optimism in me.'

'When I was a small farmer tilling land, I got into a lot of debt. I went through hell, but gates of heaven are through hell,' he says.

Capt. Gopinath converted a barren piece of land to set up a farm for ecologically sustainable silkworm rearing and won a Rolex Laureate Award in 1996. From then on, the serial entrepreneur in Capt. Gopinath kicked in, as he floated one business after another.

In 1997, Gopinath co-founded Deccan Aviation, a charter helicopter service. In 2003, he went on to establish Air Deccan, a low cost airline, and in 2009, he started Deccan 360—a freight flight business.

'When I started Air Deccan or Cargo or the helicopter company, I didn't have any money. Just the belief that I could do it was overpowering. I threw caution to the wind. It was energy, optimism, and belief that led me.'

Air Deccan merged with Kingfisher Airlines in 2007. Capt. Gopinath chronicles his meeting with the promoter of Kingfisher Airlines in his book, *Simply Fly*, where he elucidates Vijay Mallya's forthright approach in expressing his interest to buy out the airline.

Excerpts from the book:

He said, 'Gopi, you are from Bengaluru. I am from Bengaluru. Why do we need two airlines?' I promptly replied, 'Vijay, we are very different individuals. We have different philosophies, outlooks on life, and styles of functioning. How would it help to erase our individual borderlines and identities?' He suggested working together as one airline so as to avoid eating into each other's market share. He said he would like to invest in my airline. No word-mincer, Vijay spoke as if he wanted to buy me out. He would call the new airline Kingfisher Airlines. I said, 'Yes, it's not a bad idea, but I need to think about it. If we can't make a single airline through your investment in Deccan, I am sure we could collaborate. We could share our engineering and other resources.'

When I came out, Kiran Rao asked me, 'What do you make of it?' I said, 'I don't think it's going to work. We are two very different people.' I left it at that. My whole dream was to build this airline and not to make money for myself. I could have sold the business and retired on a fat compensation, and had that happened, the entire history of Indian aviation might then have been different, as would the course of my life.

'…I returned to my own real world and was seized with the faith reposed in me as chief executive of the company. I recalled my mandate: that the challenge of creating something is worth striving for, living for, and dying for. It had been my dream to achieve that, and I had sold the dream to a team of people. It did not take me long to say "No" to the overture. Kingfisher Airlines was born in its avatar because I said no. Otherwise, within six months Deccan would have been reborn as Kingfisher Airlines.'

However, Captain would eventually have to give in. Deccan went through a period of turbulence and uncertainty. The airline was losing money; flights were getting cancelled, delayed. Employees were quitting. An airline needs skilled people apart from high capital. There was a crisis almost at every front—financial, technical, and human resources.

'We lost pilots and engineers to competition. One morning I received the news that our Ahmedabad–Bengaluru flight had to be cancelled because the pilot and engineer had left and joined Kingfisher Airlines. On another day, fifteen co-pilots resigned en-masse and joined Indian Airlines,' Captain Gopinath writes in his book.

FAILURE TO CONVINCE

There was immense pressure from all sides on Capt. Gopinath to sell the airline. Investors, board members, and other stake holders were looking to Capt. Gopinath to get them the returns on their investment. There was a sense of impatience emanating from all sides, and Gopinath succumbed.

Your business plan, vision, and implementation might be extraordinary, but often, in our enthusiasm and passion, we tend to overlook something as integral as whether those who are with us see our dream.

'There were various kinds of pressures; we had not broken even, and investors were putting pressure on us. I did not show the same fierceness as I should have, and somewhere I think I should have,' he laments.

By that time the airline, he says, had achieved 'everything'.

'But people who had invested had not made money. They were saying, "We believe you, we are following you, but will we get returns?"'

It was an overwhelming decision, but Gopinath had to make it. The choice was to pursue his dream, or to work for everyone who had bought into his dream.

'There was physical pressure from the board; people were saying maybe it's my ego that's preventing me from selling because I wanted to control the company. These people had power over me. I thought it might be better to give in, because even if my dream dies, the investors will make money.'

Picking the right investor, the right partner in a business, is one of the most crucial decisions an entrepreneur has to make. The key is to find this mythical person who shares your dream, vision, and understands numbers as well—someone who practically does not exist. Eventually, it does come down to the one question: How long can you stay afloat alone?

'When you are desperate, you take money from anyone. You might not get a dream partner, but wherever you have a choice, you should pick your partner carefully regardless of the pressure. And sometimes when you do choose (an investor or a partner) with utmost caution, people can change after they have invested the money,' he says.

While Gopinath failed in his own eyes, as he saw his dream crumble, his peers saw him as an astute businessman who was ruthless, and who took the 'right' decision at the right time.

'It depends on how you define success to yourself: You might have failed in the eyes of others and at other times the world feels you have succeeded, but in your mind you know you have failed. When I merged the airline with Kingfisher, there was pressure to sell. I need not have succumbed to the pressure but I did and I merged it. In the eyes of the world I was smart because I sold it at the right time and made a lot of money.'

Gopinath's dream was to make an everyman's airline, to make flying affordable for all. Its logo showed two palms joined together to signify a bird flying. The tagline was 'Simplifly', to say that it was now possible for the common man to fly. Air Deccan was the first airline in India to fly to tier-2 cities from metros. The dream of Captain Gopinath was to enable every Indian to fly at least once in his or her lifetime.

Kingfisher Airlines merged with Air Deccan in December, 2007. Vijay Mallya acquired a 26 percent stake in Air Deccan's parent company, Deccan Aviation. Air Deccan was rechristened as Kingfisher Red. Four years later, in September 2011, Mallya announced closing of the airline citing that he didn't believe in the low cost model anymore.

'To lay people I was like God because I made flying affordable. They felt they owned the airline—it became a people's airline. They felt let down. The businessmen said he (Captain Gopinath) is the smartest guy who made the most of the opportunity. All the investors made huge money. But deep within I felt the extinguishing of a dream. Because Mallya changed the model. In hindsight, it was a mistake to sell the airline,' says Captain Gopinath nearly a year after the model that he pioneered ceased to exist.

FAILED MY EMPLOYEES

When Captain Gopinath embarked on his next entrepreneurial venture, the logistics business, he says, he had the biggest investor. 'Reliance was looking at getting into logistics and

I was looking for a strategic partner. I knew it required a lot of funding.'

He managed to convince investors of the need for a logistics business in India. The plan was robust; the market was waiting to be explored. Captain was convinced that a good logistics delivery system could strengthen the backbone of the Indian economy. Investors bought into his vision.

'But something went wrong in the relationship with Reliance. The other partner pulled out. In that sense I was a failure—I was not able to capture their imagination to continue the partnership which affected the rollout of the business. When Reliance came in, there was a huge noise in the market, everybody was falling over to invest; but when they (Reliance) decided to discontinue further investments, it affected the business. Employees had followed me like a messiah, and I felt I was not in position to fulfil their dreams. In that sense I was a failure. I had set out to achieve something and I had failed.'

In Hindsight

But would Capt. Gopinath weigh his decisions more carefully in hindsight? Perhaps becoming a serial entrepreneur requires a lot more than optimism, vision, and energy. The solution, however, is not as lucid in entrepreneurship.

'Sometimes knowledge creates fear and forces us to conform. You have a pre-set idea, that this is the way to do it. In life it might help to use that knowledge. But as an entrepreneur, it might be the biggest cause of failure. The fact is that you are trying to discover something, explore an unknown territory. If you keep knocking on the door of the best guru or the most successful businessmen to get an idea validated before you begin your journey, it is not bound to get you any success, because he is not seeing what you are seeing. He might be a great man, but genius is nothing but the art of following something you believe in. You find courage as you go along. When you embark on a journey and stake everything in that, obviously many will perish. But it is necessary to embark on a journey. "One does not discover new lands without consenting to lose sight of the shore for a very long time." If you are going on a ship—the fact that you don't want to lose sight of the land, will always keep you closer to land. If you want to see new things, you have to leave the shore.'

'There is this hunger for taking a dangerous plunge. Where you are only looking at light at the end of the tunnel, you are so consumed by the fact that you believe in your own dream that you mindlessly embark, I think that is the only way to success, while that causes failure but that is also the only way to success. The idea of an airline, of launching it when I had no money, the idea possessed me and I just went ahead and did it. I consulted how I could do it in a better manner. But embarking on a journey is born out of a dream, heart—every time.'

Captain is planning to fly again and launch another domestic airline. When I asked him, 'Why? What drives you?', he replied by quoting 'Ulysses' from Tennyson—'To strive, to seek, to find, and not to yield.'

WHY I FAILED

- Over optimism and not looking at the shadows
- Headlong rush in to starting ventures and finding investors
- Could communicate the vision of the dream, but failed to keep the conviction of all in the vision intact

Advice

- If I had gone through a logical process, I wouldn't have done many of the things, because I would be weighing out the obstacles. I was not ready to listen to anyone. Leadership is the ability to understand what your own inadequacies are and surround yourself with people that are better than you

* PS: Advice and reason for failure is author's takeaway from Captain's journey

*'For me, my struggle was a choice
I made'*

SABYASACHI MUKHERJEE

You have to deserve to wear a Sabyasachi. His clothes speak to those who they wish to. Sabyasachi Mukherjee, the young designer from Kakinara, started from nothing, went through a long period of intense self-questioning, followed by burst of fame. When his class at NIFT was designing evening gowns, he was the only one working with Indian designs. He says, he has always been the one to choose a 'wild romance' over a 'tepidly happy existence'. Sabyasachi has been lauded as the fresh voice in Indian fashion.

WHEN THE MIND IS WITHOUT FEAR

A failure of the mind can be one of the most devastating, challenging experiences of a lifetime. The point when your mind stops seeing, sensing, believing. There is darkness all around and all you can see is a deep, black hole. Several situations could push one into that state of limbo where you could spend days just staring at the ceiling and not leave your confines for months. The country's most celebrated fashion designer, whose designs have a soul and speak myriad languages, Sabyasachi Mukherjee, went through such a phase not too long ago. He felt stifled, without a voice, a thought to share.

'I went through four years of severe depression. For eight months I wouldn't get out of my room, I would just lay there and stare at the ceiling.'

This was the Sabyasachi of the early nineties when Sabyasachi's middle-class sensibilities and his family pressured him into taking up an Economic, Statistics, Mathematics course in St Xaviers college, Kolkata—a course that was suffocating his sensibilities in every way.

That's what most middle-class Indians did and still do. If they were conventionally bright, studying science was the only way to move forward and get out of the middle-class drudgery.

Sabyasachi grew up in an industrial town of Kakinara near the old French colony of Chandanagore in West Bengal. The non-descript town of Kakinara was far, far away from the glittering world of fashion that Sabyasachi would later take literally like a storm. Kakinara had one or two broken cinema halls, overcrowded buses, and ferry or cycle rickshaw were the only modes of transport.

'One of my assistants is from Chandanagore, and he was saying that the town is really modern now because there is a Levi's store there,' he says with a hint of amusement and affection. Sabyasachi grew up with the belief that you have to anchor yourself with good education. And gradually that became the core of his existence.

His family of doctors and Professors of literature was a classic middle class Bengali family. A respectable career for Sabyasachi would have to be in engineering, education, medicine, or an allied field. While Sabyasachi was an all-rounder in school, his interests lay in technology, science, and literature. He was equally inclined towards sports as he was towards poetry and drama. He was indeed the 'golden boy' who would make the family proud. Sabya, as he is affectionately called, could not do anything wrong.

'I was not hardworking; I was good at studies, because I was intelligent and sensitive. I was a role model for a lot of kids.'

He was in the fourth standard, around eight or nine years old, when he wrote his first script for a play. The standard practice was that the teachers would direct, but Sabyasachi was given the permission to direct. He did the costumes, makeup, direction, and that's perhaps when those around him realized that Sabyasachi had exceptional leadership qualities.

'My leadership qualities made me popular, or unpopular,' he says.

His creative pursuits were not restricted to the school premises alone. Summer and winter vacations were often spent in the big city, Kolkata. Sabyasachi would organize concerts on the streets of Kolkata. He was twelve or thirteen and was able to direct and motivate children older than him. It's then that Sabyasachi's creative and entrepreneurial skills were coming to the fore. He would use sketch pens as eyeliners.

It was in Kolkata that he dabbled in theatre, music, make-up, and design. Tickets for the concerts he organized were sold at 25 paise.

AND THE HEAD IS HELD HIGH

But Sabyasachi did not know that he'd end up a part of the fashion industry, though he had forever, since he could remember, sketched actresses in evening gowns on the back of almost any piece of paper he would get. Fashion was not considered as a career; there was no access to any fashion press, anyway very limited in those days in Kakinara. There were barely a handful of fashion designers to speak of.

In the mind of Sabyasachi 's family, the fashion world did not really exist. Sabyasachi's fierce sense of responsibility towards his sister, who is younger to him by seven years, his parents, and his much grounded upbringing did not let him pursue something that appeared beyond his reach.

'I was from a middle-class family, there was no fashion week, there was nothing written about fashion, there was only NIFT (National Institute of Fashion Technology) in

Delhi. Fashion was a dream for me. I dreamt big, but was also always seeped in reality. I did not grow up in a fantasy land to pursue something beyond my reach.'

'My parents had decided that either it would be engineering (chemical, civil, electrical), or I had to get into a medical school. Though my mother comes from a government arts college. I even contemplated hotel management, but my parents did not even think that hotel management was an option.'

ARRANGED MARRIAGE OR A WILD ROMANCE

His father was an engineer and worked in the wool combing industry. It was when the family moved to Kolkata and Sabyasachi enrolled into Xaviers for his degree, that Sabyasachi had a revelation.

It became apparent to Sabyasachi that he was running away from what he was destined to do. He was making a choice that would never make him truly happy. He knew that with a science or finance degree he would have a 'tepidly happy existence', but Sabyasachi wanted a wild romance. And a wild romance came with its highs and lows. He knew he was capable of handling that. What he didn't want, he says, was an 'arranged marriage', where you plough along until you start 'liking it'. 'You learn to like it. The pressures around you force you to and slowly it starts becoming a habit.'

What followed was a period of intense creativity and frustration. Sabyasachi went through depression at a time when it was still an alien disease for middle-class Indians. Psychiatrists were consulted as Sabyasachi went on for months without meeting or talking to anyone. It was a period of agonizing loneliness. Nobody understood him, not even his parents, and he began to give up hope.

But rooted in ground realities, Sabyasachi knew that, he, alone, could get himself out of the situation. So he went about plotting his own failure. He walked halfway out of his Statistics exam. He knew if he did very well, his father would force him into an engineering college. The planning was strategic enough to get a decent grade to make it through NIFT (National Institute of Fashion Technology, Kolkata).

And that's where Sabyasachi rekindled his wild romance with fashion. His father was clear that he could only afford to pay for college fee and not support the extra infrastructure costs that came with a fashion degree. The family also went through a financially tumultuous period at that time. Not only was pursuing fashion a wild gamble for him, it was during this time Sabyasachi's entrepreneurial skills were truly tested.

Sabyasachi pedalled through the streets of Kolkata selling wooden jewellery, his two family helps doubling up as his assistants. He worked with photographers as a stylist, and worked through weekends for years. He also started a small modelling agency, Creative Media, around the time. 'It was a little bit of a hell hole,' he says. But Creative Media worked with the reigning divas like Celina Jaitley, Bipasha Basu, Koena Mitra, and Resham Ghosh.

Besides helping out financially, working as a student

broadened his horizons tremendously. 'I learned what to imbibe and what not to. I understood what I needed to take from that education. I realized that there was a big gap between what was being taught in school and what the market needed. My class was designing gowns; I was the only one to design an Indian outfit in my last term. I knew I needed to learn things that would help me in setting up a design house.'

As his education at NIFT got over, Sabyasachi's sense of purpose and how he wanted to achieve it also became sharper. He knew he wanted to set up a design house, and not work for a designer.

He won all the major awards at NIFT, including the confluence award, and job offers started to come in.

'We had gone through seven years of no money, four years of depression. I had dropped out of school, and had done several odd jobs. I was starting to get a little stronger, but my parents were getting desperate. When I got a job offer for a twenty five thousand rupee salary with a car, they were thrilled. Though they did not consider it respectful.'

'I refused the job—I realized that I would be manufacturing for someone else. And not design.'

Instead Sabyasachi took up an eight hundred rupee per month job in Kolkata to learn printing.

His dreams were far beyond a twenty five thousand rupee job, something his ecosystem could not really believe or understand. But by that point Sabyasachi had stopped trying to convince or get heard. He was working with dogged ambition, grit, and determination. He rejected an offer to go to university abroad. The offer came at a time when

Sabyasachi was yet to even be on an airplane. That alone could have been an incentive for many. But for Sabyasachi, the university would have taken him farther from his goal. The eight hundred rupee printing job helped him learn about textiles, a learning that would go a long way in his ambition to build a label in India.

I HAVE A DREAM

Sabyasachi did his first exhibition in partnership with a Marwari housewife in Kolkata in the early 2000s. The exhibition was a huge success, selling out in the first fifteen minutes. However, recognition of Sabyasachi's talent upset his partner considerably. She took advantage of the fact that both parties were not bound by any contractual obligations, and refused to pay, leaving Sabyasachi literally without a rupee.

Nilangi Parekh spotted him and bought all the leftover clothes designed by Sabyasachi and that's how he raised the start-up capital of twenty five thousand rupees for the Sabyasachi business.

The tailor who worked with him during his days of struggle is still with Sabyasachi. 'I told him, if you don't take salary for two months, I will make sure you are well taken care of, because I will be the biggest designer in the country. He believed me.'

Sabyasachi converted his bedroom into a tailoring workshop, while his mother's bedroom was converted into a studio. Every rupee earned was being rolled back into the business. And that's when Sabyasachi bought his first two sewing machines.

'There was no air conditioning in the apartment, no elevator in the building, and my parents apartment was on a higher floor—it was a retail nightmare. But word travelled, and we did well.'

His next breakthrough moment came when he dressed actor-model Celina Jaitley for Miss India. In 2001, Sabyasachi Mukherjee won the Femina British Council Award that took him to London for an internship with the Salisbury-based Georgina von Etzdorf.

'I was like a sponge in London. It was my first trip abroad. I learnt everything and came back far more astute, sharper about my business.'

And that was the start of his career, that he says, 'has grown so big'.

'The brand happened overnight.' In 2002, at the Indian Fashion week in Delhi, Mukherjee showed a collection that almost catapulted his status. His designs of dresses and skirts in vibrant colours with strips of embroidery were inspired by gypsies, and the prostitutes of Kolkata's infamous red light district. He added his sense of drama by adding thick black spectacles and large bindis that models wore on their forehead.

Since then, there has been no looking back for the small town boy from Kakinara who had nearly committed suicide because life had been too overbearing at one time. Like he says, 'Somewhere deep inside, you know what you are and who you are.' It was because he knew who he was and what he was capable of that he could counter circumstances and make the choices (such as not taking up the twenty five thousand rupees per month job or not going to university abroad) that he made and created his destiny.

This is just the beginning for Sabyasachi Mukherjee. Even today he remains very nonchalant about his dreams and aspirations as he quietly ploughs along. He has gone past the stage of trying to convince people, or making people see his dreams, his vision.

'I still don't want to tell people about my dreams, because people will laugh.'

'For me, I have always known. When I went to fashion week, I told my mother I would be in the papers the next day. She laughed at me.'

Currently, Sabyasachi is searching for a business partner. 'A mythical man who writes poetry and understands numbers. A man with a high EQ and IQ.'

WHY I FAILED

- There were times when I let my circumstances overwhelm me into inaction

Advice

- Every situation and circumstance can be turned around

- Be careful about the choices you make. What might be the right choice for many, may be the worst for you

- Pick your goal and you will know what to do next

- There is no substitute for hard work and perseverance

- Know who you are and what you are

- Dream big and go for it

'At Softronics, if I had succeeded in getting some domestic revenue–which I could be satisfied with–Infosys might not have been born'

NARAYANA MURTHY

Narayana Murthy, India's first technology entrepreneur, is responsible for putting India on the global map of knowledge economy. Founder of Infosys, Murthy has always led by example. His vision and implementation has cemented Infosys' position as the company credited with many firsts. Ironically, Murthy credits his accomplishments to his initial failures. He has been awarded with a Padma Shri and Padma Vibhushan. Besides being on the board of companies and his vast contribution in establishing India's credibility as service delivery provider, he is known for his philanthropy work. He is on the advisory board of the Ford Foundation and UN Foundation, among others.

The story of India's first technology entrepreneur, Narayana Murthy, is the stuff of legends of modern times. There are elements of passion, love, family, and failure, followed by phenomenal success.

His biggest lessons have come from setbacks, and from his ability to take away from difficult circumstances. The story of Narayana Murthy's failure and success is also quintessentially Indian.

There is passion, an audacity of hope, love, patriotism, hard work, and optimism tempered with realism. It was intrepidity that he thought of leveraging technology at a time in India, when even a landline telephone connection was considered a luxury. Businesses were considered brutally capitalist in a heavily socialist India. Imagination, ideas, entrepreneurship were inhibited with permissions, red tape, and bureaucracy. It was in this India of the eighties that Murthy thought of India's first company that would put India on the map of world knowledge economy. Infosys was as much a result of failure, as the vision and unwavering conviction of its founder, the legendary Narayana Murthy.

Murthy is revered in India and around the world for his entrepreneurial energy and ability to fight the demons that stymied various businesses at the time. He, along with his six engineering colleagues, started Infosys at a time when there were prohibitive government controls. The entire decade of the eighties was a 'dark hour', says Murthy. 'There was a lot of friction. Getting a telephone connection required three to five years; licenses required 18-20 months.'

His key lessons that he would go on to apply to build one of the most formidable businesses in the country came from a company he had started long before Infosys—Softronics, a company he founded in 1976. But selling software in India, the core idea of the business, was far ahead of its time. The company lasted a little over a year, and Murthy, who firmly believed that entrepreneurship was the answer to many problems plaguing India, let go of his first business venture.

'Right from the time I came back from France, I wanted to experiment with entrepreneurship. I truly believe that countries could only come out of poverty through entrepreneurship.' It was while working in France that Murthy got highly disappointed by socialist ideologies, and at the core he was of the belief that entrepreneurship could lift nations out of poverty.

While he was passionate about the idea of selling software in India and Softronics was his first venture, he did not let love for the idea and for his first company come in the way of an objective analysis of where things were going with the business.

He was quick to realize that the venture was not really taking off. He knew he wanted to be an entrepreneur and that the business had to make money eventually. The novelty of the idea was not enough to pay salaries, expand, and keep the business afloat. He also knew that the timing of Softronics was not right in terms of market acceptability. Softronics shut down barely a year later.

Murthy was cold in his analysis as he quickly realized that his first dream entrepreneurial venture was a failure. It was a business that would not take off in the near future.

'Fortunately, I had my friend Sudha (wife) to discuss it with. Both of us realized that Softronics did not look like (it was) succeeding. We did not want to go on and on. We realized there was no market for software in India at the time.'

While Murthy could have let this setback affect him in many ways—including pushing him away from entrepreneurship. He could have abandoned his dream. Lost his confidence, or just walked away, defeated and dejected. He instead took this 'opportunity', as he refers to it, to do some introspection and soul-searching.

WITH OPEN ARMS

He realized that the ability to embrace challenges, and to learn from criticism, was very important for the growth of one's aspirations and mind. There is a special emphasis that he lays on the importance of what he calls the 'correct' mindset. He spoke about the importance of the right mindset in great detail in a lecture to business school students at New York University. He said, 'A fixed mindset, creates a tendency to avoid challenges, to ignore useful negative feedback, and leads such people to plateau early and not achieve their full potential. A growth mindset leads to a tendency to embrace challenges, to learn from criticism, and such people reach even higher levels of achievement.

Murthy approached his failed start-up with the mindset to learn, absorb, and implement the learnings. It was perhaps then, for the first time, that Murthy realized that beyond the idea and the scalability of the idea, a start-up company had to get a steady revenue stream from activities that are well understood in the marketplace. 'So that it does not take too much creative energy of founders and founders can focus on creative ideas,' he says.

THE BIG IDEA

Murthy's next idea would turn out to be an important milestone for post-liberalized India and play a very significant role in putting India on the global map for its expertise in technology and services. Infosys was founded in 1981, at a time when the country was choked with excessive controls, red tape, and bureaucracy.

However, with Infosys, Murthy had the learnings from Softronics to fall back on. Moreover, his first failure had emboldened him, he had much greater confidence now in his idea and strengths. In fact, he lays much emphasis on the power of self-knowledge in bouncing back from failure. In his lecture at The Stern School (New York University), he described self-knowledge as a 'cornerstone of the Indian spiritual tradition'. It is, he said, 'the highest form of knowledge.'

'I believe this greater awareness and knowledge of oneself is what ultimately helps develop a more grounded belief in oneself, courage, determination, and, above all, humility—all qualities which enable one to wear one's success with dignity and grace.'

Murthy is considered an exemplary business leaders for several reasons—he brought in fresh business practices. Infosys pioneered the Global Delivery Model and became the first IT company from India to be listed on NASDAQ. Its employee stock options created some of India's first salaried millionaires.

With his Softronics experience, he had a much better understanding of structural strengths and weaknesses in a business model. Just as he knew that the Softronics model had inherent weaknesses, he was confident that the Infosys model of focussing on the fast growth export market in the US would be a success. It was an idea that would capitalize on India's strengths of IT talent and fill an obvious need in the export market.

'If the Government of India did not initiate reforms, we could have moved to another country. I was pretty confident about the concept,' he says.

It was during the one and half years of trying to establish Softronics when Murthy realized that it was taking an enormous amount of time and effort to get a small portion of revenues, that he decided that his next venture would have to be 'much better' at handling risk. 'We realized that we could not depend on one company or one source of revenue.'

It was in the same year that the company was founded that Infosys signed up its first client, Data Basics Corporation, in New York. Within six years, Infosys opened its first international office in Boston, US.

Infosys went on to become one of the most iconic technology companies in India. Through the journey there were periods of self-doubt, and pulls and pressures of selling the company after it had seen success. But this time Murthy believed in his vision that kept him on the path to pursue his life's purpose.

There came a time when the other founders of Infosys wanted to sell the company and it was Murthy who dared to make an offer of buying out the other founders—an offer even he couldn't fathom himself. Murthy didn't have the money, but he did have the optimism and conviction. After an hour of arguments, he was able to convince his colleagues to believe in what they had created, to not fall into the temptation of selling out before they or the company had realized its full potential. The six founders worked together towards building Infosys as a company that would be the force behind many firsts in India Inc. 'I urged them that if we wanted to create a great company, we should be optimistic and confident.'

Dividing risks is a lesson Murthy learnt when Infosys failed to retain one of the company's biggest clients. It was a Fortune-10-company, and Infosys, with revenues of five million dollars, was dependent on the company for twenty-five percent of its revenues. The loss of this client could be potentially disastrous for the recently-listed Infosys.

The customer was a tough negotiator and Infosys was pitted against other software vendors. The terms and conditions of the contract were aggressive and Murthy had to make a decision on whether to go ahead with the customer's demands or stick to the company's conviction of charging a fair price that would allow the company to invest in good people, R&D, infrastructure, technology, and training. It was a difficult decision for Murthy; there was a lot at stake financially for the company, but he was aware that by agreeing to the terms, he would be putting the company's reputation, that had been built over the years through a lot of dedication and hard work, at stake.

Murthy promised a smooth transition to the next vendor, and with that failure, he recognized the importance of diversifying risks. Infosys created a Risk Mitigation Council, and put together a de-risking strategy, according to which Infosys ensured no overdependence on any one client, technology, country, application area, or employee.

Murthy's Infosys was pioneering in many ways—from its business model, corporate governance, to setting higher standards in delivery. It became the first company to report quarterly earnings, and the first to have come up with the concept of a lead independent director. Murthy stepped down as CEO in 2002. And a lot has changed since. Infosys is no longer the poster child of Indian IT. The company that leaped ahead on the back of its focus and vision, is faltering. The Infosys model, once considered pioneering in many ways, is failing to adapt and keep pace with the newer and more competitive players in the Indian IT landscape. Then again, Murthy is no longer at the helm of the company he founded.

WHY I FAILED

- The market was not ready for the idea
- I did not have the wherewithal to create the market
- Overdependence on one company or vertical for revenues makes you vulnerable

Advice

- You have to provide time and space for ideas to implement
- Success reinforces your action and that action may not be the best
- As long as you put in an honest day's work, show entrepreneurship, and take calculated risk, you shouldn't mind failures
- You must work hard
- Your focus on implementing your ideas will keep your enthusiasm intact
- Don't mull over problems, find solutions
- Problems don't daunt people, what daunts people is being at a dead end
- Bring people with good ideas together
- Create an environment that reveres meritocracy
- Don't allow hierarchy to inhibit ideas
- Failure in some ways is much more of a lesson giver than success

'Everyone told me I was a fool to want to start a corporate hospital'

DR PRATHAP C. REDDY

Prathap C. Reddy, Chairman, Apollo Hospitals redefined healthcare in India. He corporatized healthcare in India at a time when it was strictly a government domain. Today, Apollo is one of Asia's largest health care firms—with over 50 hospitals, over a thousand pharmacies, clinics, and an insurance joint venture with Munich Health, arm of Munich Re Group.

Nothing can ever be perfect, they say. You cannot have it all. And you will have to adapt, experiment, fail, and experiment again to get it right. All these predicaments especially hold true if you are embarking on the very rocky path of entrepreneurship.

You can want to be a pioneer, but then do you have the ability to learn and unlearn simultaneously? To stay on course against all odds? To move on when it is time? To fail and realize that you have failed? To chart your own path?

The man who brought private healthcare to India managed to do all of the above and more. Dr Prathap Chandra Reddy moved back to India in 1978 from the United States of America. The concept of private healthcare was alien to India at the time and Dr Reddy wanted to bring about a dynamic change in a sector which had always been the domain of the government. There were no private hospitals, just small nursing homes, at the time.

Dr Reddy was a practising cardiologist in the US, living the American dream, a life almost all Indians aspired for. While America was considered the land that helped make the impossible, possible, India was fraught with tight controls. From food to amenities, everything was rationed. Government was all pervasive, permeating every aspect of our life. 1970s was a post-Nehru India; India's policies were heavily socialist and protectionist. It was Indira Gandhi's India, when banks were nationalized and more socialist economic and industrial policies enacted. India was the poster child for post-World War II socialism in the Third World. Industries were subjected to crushing regulation that very nearly stifled industry and innovation. The Industries Act of 1951 required all businesses to get a license from the government before they could launch, expand, or even change their product strategy.

Foreign investment was subject to grinding restrictions. The economy was driven to the brink. While Japan's economy grew ten times faster than India's between 1950 and 1973, India's economy crawled along at two percent per year between 1973 and 1987. Policymakers continued to be in denial, as they termed the painfully slow growth as the 'Hindu Rate of Growth'. The then Prime Minister, Indira Gandhi, in an address at the Institute of Economic Growth in Delhi, November 16, 1983, had commented on the perception of India around the world: 'Those in India and abroad, who are ideologically opposed to the very concept of democratic socialism, comment caustically that planning has produced more economists than economic change, more reports than results.'

'The planless or rolling period between 1977 and 1979 was a chastening experience,' she had said, reflecting on the state of the economy, and the perception battles that she and her government were fighting.[1]

Dr Prathap C. Reddy was probably one of the first people to have convinced Indira Gandhi of the role of private sector in healthcare. Dr Reddy was a cardiologist who had decided to also become an entrepreneur to bring in the best healthcare practices of the world to India. His agility in adapting so quickly to the Indian way is striking. There were several

1 Source: Indira Gandhi: Selected speeches and writings (1982-1984)

frustrations and failures, but he persevered, and pursued relentlessly. The wait period for permissions for licenses, land acquisition, or to import equipment extended over days and years. Permissions were given and revoked. Trips between the National Capital and Chennai were near weekly. Dr Reddy learned quickly that the Indian business environment was actually hostile to business. Profits and entrepreneurship were the anathema in the country.

'When I came back to India, Charan Singh was the prime minister (1979-1980). I wrote to him that I wanted to start a corporate body (a private healthcare company) and list it. I understand that he just tore it and threw it. He was also the finance minister. I spoke to his secretary and asked him about my letter. He said: "Dr Reddy, we don't clear waste paper baskets and it has gone into the waste paper basket."'

'I wanted to ask Charan Singh why he would do that! My problem was I couldn't explain in Hindi. At the time it sounded like such an alien idea. There were so many obstacles. Nobody attempted an organization like hospitals with all the features in it. Nobody understood the capital it needed and the permissions it required. First permission needed was to import medical equipment—for each equipment you needed to file 12 applications, and we imported 367 items,' he recalls, after spending nearly three decades in building one of the most trusted brands in healthcare in India today.

Apollo hospitals has grown to become one of Asia's largest integrated healthcare organizations with over 9000 beds across 50 hospitals, more than 1200 pharmacies, and over

100 diagnostic clinics. Apollo has played a significant role in opening up healthcare for the private sector and changing the dynamics of the healthcare industry in India.

When Dr Reddy failed to make headway with the government in his first attempt, he decided to wait it out—he waited for the Congress to come back to power. And while he waited, he also started working on laying the foundation of the institution. He went back to the US and sought advice from his colleagues. 'I went to Thomas Junior hospital in Nashville; I didn't even have a visiting card. I sent in a note to speak to the one of the key surgeons there. He echoed my sentiments on the state of healthcare in government hospitals. Patients were not getting the care they wanted.

The irony was that in India, there were many who were willing to come forward to lend support to a charitable hospital, but not a private hospital. 'I had friends, family, patients who would have given Rs 10 crore to start a charitable hospital. Everyone told me I was being a fool to be giving up a lucrative practice and putting so much money in a hospital.'

'"You have a lovely practice, everyone is coming to you in town. You think you alone can change the entire health structure? You are doing an impossible thing," they would say.'

Dr Reddy started out of a room on top of a garage which was his first Apollo office. A change in the Indian administration helped. 'Venkatraman was the finance minister (R. Venkatraman was the finance minister between 1980-1982; succeeded by Pranab Mukherjee). Venkatraman gave Dr Reddy hope when he said, 'As the finance minister, the first signature I put would be on Apollo hospitals to raise money.'

Prime Minister Indira Gandhi had got a glimpse into what Dr Reddy wanted to bring into India, when she came to Chennai to visit Maruthur Gopalan Ramachandran in the hospital. MGR, as he is popularly known, was the Chief Minister of Tamil Nadu from 1977 to December 1987.

'Only two of us (Dr Prathap Reddy and Prime Minister Indira Gandhi) were in the lift. Indira Gandhi believed me and gave me a chance.'

But permissions required and regulations controlling every sector were as stifling as before. First set of permissions was to import medical equipment and second set was to list the company on the bourses.

While the Prime Minister had given her nod, the recommendation also had to come from the state government, followed by the director general of health services, and subsequently around twelve different government bodies.

It was exhaustive and tiresome to say the least. For Dr Reddy that was only part of the battle: 'Every Thursday I would come back to Delhi and go back on Friday or Saturday. I did this for three to six months continuously.'

Dr Reddy also needed permission to tap the market for funds. Banks were not allowed to give loans to hospitals.

'In Bombay they laughed when I said I wanted to list the share.'

But by then Dr Reddy had acclimatized himself to people laughing at his plans and their disparaging comments. After many, many meetings and knocking on several doors, he met a trader in Bombay who was willing to help in taking Apollo public. 'I met a dalal in Bombay. He wanted to see my office in Chennai, and I was working out of a one-room office on top of a garage. I brought him home. He wouldn't even drink water in my house before signing business (business document). He agreed to underwrite the issue.'

Apollo was the first healthcare issue that went public. The first day it was subscribed by 35-36 percent.

Since banks were not allowed to give loans to hospitals, Dr Reddy had to reinvent the wheel, once again. He went back to the Finance Minister, R. Venkataraman, who directed Dr Reddy to approach the Industrial Development Bank of India. At the time, IDBI was constituted under the Industrial Development Bank of India Act, 1964, as a Development Financial Institution. It was regarded as a Public Financial Institution and continued to serve as a DFI for nearly 40 years, till 2004.

IDBI said they thought the 'project was very unique and that they would like to fund it'.

'Venkataraman was visiting Chennai. He asked me to get there towards the end of his day, at around eight, to sign on the permission document. But in between that time, someone in the department of banking had written on the permission document that funding the project will invite impeachment. So Venkataraman had a blank face and told me, "This can't be done . . . you meet me in Delhi in a week".'

During that week, there was a Cabinet shuffle, and Venkataraman was moved to the post of Defence Minister, and the current President of India, Pranab Mukherjee, took charge as Finance Minister.

The current Prime Minister Manmohan Singh, was the deputy governor of the Reserve Bank of India at the time. Singh was RBI Governor between 1982 and 1985.

Dr Reddy was asked to wait for the finance minister's verdict, 'Indira Gandhi (Prime Minister) had approved it, he (the banking secretary) said, let's see what the minister will say.'

The elusive letter of permission came; the finance minister had allowed Apollo to borrow fifty percent from banks and fifty percent from foreign exchange for import of medical equipment.

But it did not end there. Dr Reddy had to go for credit authorization to the Reserve Bank of India. In the meantime, the Credit Authorization Officer had changed. 'He said, "Why should I go 360 degrees to give you permission?"' The Governor clearly told Dr Reddy that he couldn't do much since this was the prerogative of the Credit Authorization Officer.

Dr Reddy was now reeling under an overwhelming sense of defeat. He was at the airport, heading back to Chennai, feeling demoralized, when he bumped into the then Minister of Civil Aviation, A.P. Sharma, at the airport.

'Sharma suggested we go to Delhi right away and knock on Pranab Mukherjee's door. It was a quarter past eleven in the night when we reached Mukherjee's residence. I told Pranab Mukherjee: "Tomorrow the Deputy Governor is going for two weeks. My whole project will be derailed." He said to me, it will be done. And asked me to get to the Reserve Bank Building at twelve noon the next day.'

Reddy took the first flight to Mumbai. It was monsoons in Mumbai, rains were pounding with all their fervour and gusto, delaying Dr Reddy by forty-five minutes. He reached at quarter to one, and looked on as the Credit Authorization Officer signed on the permission document permitting Apollo to raise funds from banks and foreign exchange, and said: 'You know why I am doing this.'

Finally Dr Reddy's ordeal of cutting through layers of bureaucracy and red tape to get permissions to build a state-of-the-art hospital ended. As a deluge of emotions flooded his mind, he received a call from finance minister, saying: 'You were not there at 12 pm.'

There were several, several times and moments when Dr Prathap Reddy was compelled through inefficiencies of the system, criticisms, bureaucracy to give up—from the time when construction of the hospital in Chennai was halted for a year and a half for land approval issues to when a realtor in Bombay offered Dr Reddy double the money for to sell the hospital property. But Dr Reddy persevered. For him, Apollo was not just a business. He had found his purpose, and it was that sense of purpose that kept going against all odds. He always saw the big picture, the challenges kept driving his vision to provide people of India with better healthcare.

His journey was about building a dream.

'I never thought of quitting. This is not the end of the road, because I never followed a path. This is a continuous journey; I don't know when the journey will end.'

WHY I FAILED

- My idea seemed grand and ahead of its time
- I wanted to bring a private player in a government-controlled sector
- Policy uncertainty and bureaucracy added to enormous delay

Advice

- Adapt to change
- Persevere, persist, and work hard
- Chase your dream
- Believe in your vision
- Know everything there is to know in your industry

'I was in a state of shock for almost a month'

SUNIL ALAGH

Sunil Alagh is one of the most recognized names in branding and marketing in India. He was managing director and CEO, Britannia Industries Ltd where he spent 14 years, between 1989 and 2003. He is known for some of Britannia's most memorable campaigns, including 'Eat Healthy, Think Better'. Alagh's open battle with Britannia was one of the first high profile public exits in corporate India. He currently serves as an advisor to Warbug Pincus LLC, an independent non-executive director of Gati Limited, and director of Tamara Capital Advisors Pvt. Ltd. He is also president of All India Management Association and is on the Board of Governors of IIM, Bangalore. Alagh is chairman of SKA Advisors, a firm he founded. His story is a fascinating insight into the constant turf battles between promoters and professionals.

You are Fired!

Why do CEOs get fired? Research or surveys have thrown up several theories and reasons and contrary to popular perception, it is not always because a quarterly target was missed or there was a slump in profits.

A study by LeadershipIQ.com interviewing 1087 board members from 286 public, private, business, and healthcare organizations shows that reasons could vary from mismanaging change, ignoring customers, tolerating low performers, too much talk and no action, and being in denial—either not recognizing the bad news or just being very far away from the realties.

Unlike in the West, especially the US, where fired CEOs or top leadership have been open about the reasons for their exit, such exits have been fairly underplayed in India. Very rarely have Indian CEOs or top leadership been asked to leave publicly—companies are most often conspicuously vague and politically correct about such exits and the awfully guarded Indian mindset prohibits a public display of failure.

How often have we heard of an Indian CEO publicly accept failure? When the CEO of Groupon Andrew Mason wrote a memo to the employees explaining the reasons why he was fired from the company he founded, he was refreshingly blunt and honest. He wrote: 'For those who are concerned about me, please don't be—I love Groupon, and I'm terribly proud of what we've created. I'm OK with having failed at this part of the journey. If Groupon was Battletoads, it would be like I made it all the way to the Terra Tubes without dying on my first ever play through. I am so lucky to have had the opportunity to take the company this far with all of you. I'll now take some time to decompress (FYI, I'm looking for a good fat camp to lose my Groupon 40, if anyone has a suggestion), and then maybe I'll figure out how to channel this experience into something productive.'

He admitted that he was responsible for Groupon's slide— the company's stock price had come down to a quarter of its listing price at the time of Mason's exit in February, 2013. While Mason's confession letter to his employees was applauded as a standard of honesty, Indian business environment would perhaps be far less accepting of such confessions.

India's corporate culture stems from the society that lays too much emphasis on success and brutally condemns failure. It is because of this stigma associated with accepting defeat and failure that public admissions are so rare.

WHY ME?

Corporate battles in India are more or less confined to the boardrooms, if at all. So when Sunil Alagh, the very flamboyant and successful CEO and managing director of Britannia Industries, was asked to leave rather flagrantly, it was shocking, not only for Alagh himself, but for analysts, media, and the corporate world.

One, because CEOs and MDs rarely get sacked, especially when they have spent a near lifetime with a company and have been successful in driving the growth of the company.

Secondly, in India, such battles between promoters and employees are rarely so blatant.

'I was in a state of shock for almost a month,' says Alagh. His ouster from the company in 2003 was quite unceremonious to say the least. It was a public battle between an employee and a giant, fast moving consumer goods company. The first of its kind ever witnessed in India's corporate history. Sunil Alagh found himself pitted against the promoters of the company he had spent nearly decades with. A company he had helped build. It was a lone battle against one of India's oldest business families. There were allegations and charges. There was passion and loyalty. And in the end there was an immense sense of failure. Failure for not having seen it coming, and for believing that the dream run could never end.

Alagh's giant Britannia cookie had crumbled—just like that. His career graph was a heady mix of power, fame, and success. Britannia had climbed to the number two spot in the most trusted brands list under his leadership. Alagh was in-tune with the customer, and was the key force behind the repositioning of Britannia as a healthy brand. The tagline, 'Eat healthy, think better' was Alagh's, he says. Britannia's blockbuster products, such as Tiger, Pure Magic, Marie were introduced when Alagh was leading the company.

So, essentially, Alagh did what a leader ought to do for a company. He pushed revenues, sales, growth, innovation, volumes, and built the brand.

He says, 'Every promoter usually tells his managers to run the company as if it is their own.' And that Alagh did very well, which ultimately led to his fall.

Within years he *was* the face of Britannia. He was one of the key forces behind the deal with a French company, Groupe Danone SA, that gave Britannia a big push in the highly competitive and crowded FMCG market.

Alagh is the quintessential Type A personality: driven, aggressive, and a go-getter. He set bigger goals and accomplished them.

'If the market is growing at 10 percent, I must grow at 11, is what I would say to myself,' he says.

Were his bosses happy with the growth he had brought to the company? Probably, yes. But as Alagh grew as large as the brand he nurtured, he ruffled many feathers. While he got the job done, he probably alienated many along the way.

Alagh was asked to leave the company on charges of financial irregularities, especially in regard to Alagh's personal expenses. Britannia Industries communicated to the stock exchanges that Alagh 'as a managing director, had conducted himself in a manner clearly incompatible and inconsistent with the duties and responsibilities he owed as managing director...'

'When they want to get you, they can get to you for all sorts of things—they can get to you over trivial technical details which were at that time considered as unwritten perks of CEOs. In any event, all expenses were audited by internal and external auditors and reported to the Board,' Alagh says, nine years after his exit from the company.

Alagh says, he intuitively knew something was wrong a year before he was asked to leave. In 2002, senior vice president, Nikhil Sen, was elevated to chief operating officer by chairman, Nusli Wadia.

'The person below me was being offered my position. It (the plan to sack Alagh) was going on for nine months. I found out in January.' Alagh was asked to leave in May 2003.

'I was quite at a loss. As a person you begin to reassess relationships. Why is that people you thought you did so much for are letting you down.'

Was it greed that led to Alagh's fall? Or was it because Alagh had become so big that he became an irritant to the promoters? Alagh says it was the latter that led to his ouster. Concept of professional CEOs was fairly new to India at that time. Most family-run companies preferred to hold on to the reins to keep complete control over the company. Sometimes there is a complete disconnect between the vision of the CEO and the promoter which could also hasten the CEO's exit.

STAND BY ME

Nearly a decade later, Alagh says, his biggest learning has been not to blame others when things go wrong.

'Ultimately it is your fault in putting your trust in the Mir Jaffar's around you. You are always stabbed in the back by those close to you. An enemy always shoots you from the front and you are generally well prepared for this.'

The first month after the exit was a period of intense questioning and self-doubt.

'I was wrongly dismissed with little savings and a life ahead of me—boy, was I depressed!'

'If you don't have anyone around you, something like this can destroy you.'

It was his wife, two daughters and a few friends that provided him with the support structure he needed.

After a month of intense pain, Alagh started to get back on his feet. He tapped into his network that he had developed outside the company he had worked for, and he tapped into himself—his strengths and energy..

'You get yourself together and decide that you will not let yourself get destroyed by something like that.'

While Alagh's integrity had been questioned, his capabilities had been proven by Britannia's performance. As he started out on his own, one of his first clients was the largest biotechnology company in India today, Biocon. Its legendary founder, Kiran Mazumdar-Shaw, approached Alagh for a more retail-focussed branding strategy for the drugs manufactured by her company.

Biocon was followed by global private equity majors, Warburg Pincus and Actis. They sought Alagh's expertise in marketing and branding. After spending thirty years in the FMCG space, marketing of financial products and services was a completely new domain for him. But that did not deter him—his confidence in him had shaken a bit, but within he was also now acutely aware of his strengths and weaknesses.

His enthusiasm was back as he took up opportunities where he felt he could add value.

'My weakness was my trust in people. Strengths are your

work. And your colleagues or clients are associates—not family, that was a learning for me.'

It was early opportunities offered by Biocon, Warburg Pincus, and Actis that helped him regain confidence and start again. In hindsight, Alagh says he could have left Britannia five years earlier. He has moved on since, with the biggest failure and possibly the biggest success of his career behind him. Alagh is currently founder and chairman of SKA Advisors, a company offering marketing and branding solutions.

WHY I FAILED

- I ran the company like it was my own
- I had a good feeling about Britannia. If it could happen to me, it could happen to anyone. You are told to run the company like it's your own, when you do behave like that, perhaps it upsets a lot of people

Advice

- Plan your exit/retirement early

- Get your finances sorted five years before your scheduled retirement/exit age

- Develop a network based on performance and credibility that you can fall back on in times of need. A mere network will not be of much use

- Constantly reassess your level of motivation and dedication to an organization and always seek broader horizons. This will give you the courage to deal with unanticipated and unexpected changes in your life. Very often these changes ultimately turn out to be for the better

'But I know I will come back;
Subhash Ghai will not die without
being what he wants to be'

SUBHASH GHAI

Subhash Ghai or the erstwhile 'Punjab University ka Hero', is the first filmmaker to corporatize film making and also the first to have dabbled in film education. A storyteller since he was ten years old, his passion for cinema transcends across genres. The man behind iconic blockbusters, such as, *Khalnayak, Pardes, Saudagar, Kalicharan*, with his film school, Whistling Woods International, he hopes to set new standards for education in arts and film making.

BELIEVING IN YOURSELF WHEN OTHERS DON'T

'I hate the Subhash Ghai of the last decade,' says the legendary filmmaker, the first man to corporatize filmmaking in India on the website of his company, Mukta Arts. After spending thirty years in Indian cinema and giving Bollywood some of its iconic hits, Ghai today sounds almost poignant, tired and battle scarred. It has been a trial by failure. His life story could have been an inspirational film script, I tell him, as he talks about the various setbacks and failures that have made Subhash Ghai.

He is refreshingly honest and open as he begins to explain 'Why he Failed.' Each failure, Ghai says, has had a huge impact on his emotions and mind. And each time the process of realization and learning was painfully slow.

Sometimes life's circumstances, at times his own ambition, overoptimism and love failed him. But each time, Ghai came back smarter, sharper, stronger, and more aware.

'Each time I failed at something, I felt I was pushed totally into a corner. When you fall, the first thing you do is get up, unless you are dead. You get up, you straighten yourself, and then you turn. This moment teaches you so much. Falling gives you a new kind of thinking, a new kind of power.'

It has been this power that has kept Subhash Ghai running breathlessly for thirty years. The first showman of India was a loner until he first moved to Mumbai to try his luck at cinema.

As a child he had to often shuttle between families of relatives since he didn't really have a home to call his own.

His parents were divorced and that meant Ghai would look towards his extended family for comfort and support. But as Ghai speaks about his childhood, he does not dwell too much on what he did not have, his optimism comes through as he chooses to see the rainbows over the dark clouds: 'I was brought up house to house. But I thank God I am not a son of one parent. All my relatives raised me; I spent time with multiple families. If I would have grown up in one family, I would have been an exact replica of my parents. My whole upbringing had a lot of variety. There were no fixed set of values that I grew up with, and that has been reflected in my films.'

Ghai's romanticism reflects in his cinema and in the reflection of his life's experiences. His childhood was markedly different from that of his peers: he did not grow up in the comfort of stability; instead, his childhood was indubitable with loneliness and perhaps a constant sense of insecurity. There was a deep void, which was apparent to him as it was to others, and he made every effort to fill it.

'I had a fractured family. In my mind I saw myself as a failure child.'

But his resilience, love for life and adventure did not lead him down the path of self-pity. His childhood was about longing but never brooding. Even when every child of the hostel would go home for two months during the holidays, and he would be the only one left behind with a guard and a cook, he did not indulge his vulnerabilities. It was during those long periods of isolation and loneliness, that the writer, the storyteller in Ghai came to fore. It is this time that helped Ghai build his 'inner strength', preparing him for the slew of failures in Bollywood—an industry, known to be particularly difficult to outsiders, and Ghai, son of a Chartered Accountant, was an outsider.

'When I was alone in the hostel, I used the opportunity to broaden myself. I started singing, doing drama. I became a hero of the hostel. "Punjab University ka hero." I became a top dramatist. I put all my energies into creativity. I would write plays, stories. I would gather kids from the area and make music. We would learn classical music. I would think how could anyone take pity on me. I would use every failure, every vacuum to my advantage. While I was a loner, I was also a hero.'

Ghai was exceptionally good at drama, theatre, and music—it was while directing a play or singing or making music that he felt alive and truly fulfilled.

Filmmaking was not even considered a career, Ghai was expected to follow his father's footsteps and spend his life deciphering numbers.

'One day, when I passed my BCom, my father told me to join CA (Chartered Accountancy). I told him I want to join the movies. My father always believed that I was good at nothing. He always thought of me to be a failure. I never shared my success in all that I had done in school and college with him. I let him think that I was good at nothing. To my shock, he told me there was an FTII (Film and Television Institute of India, the largest and the oldest film school in the country) advertisement in the paper and that I should go get trained. And come back after failing.'

Later, Ghai discovered, that it his college principal who had shown conviction in his talent and had convinced the father.

'The principal told my father that don't destroy Subhash's talent.' It would be that conversation that would set the course for Ghai's destiny. His years at FTII (Film and Television Institute of India) was a period of self discovery, learning and absorbing. It was here that he realized that he, too, could succeed at something.

'FTII broadened my mind further. I have always believed that it is never the teacher who teaches, but the student who learns.'

However, his faith in himself would be questioned again as he embarked on another journey, this time as a filmmaker. He graduated from FTII as one of the top three actors out of ten thousand students. The very dapper, first star of Indian cinema, Rajesh Khanna, was with him among the top three of the class.

THE FIVE YEAR JINX

It took Ghai nearly five years to get his first break. When Ghai came to the industry, along with the late Rajesh Khanna, he wanted to become an actor. There was no doubt about his acting prowess, but, as in most cases, things didn't quite go as planned for Ghai.

FTII gave him the confidence, the skills, but no college or educational institute really prepares you to deal with constant rejections. It is particularly frustrating when you know you have it in you to accomplish what you have set out for.

But, as he would realize later, talent is perhaps only 30 percent of the battle, the rest is perception and, the ability to take people along. To be able to shine, yet not threaten. It's a tight rope walk, and there are many who fall off while trying to strike that elusive balance. Ghai had proved his acting skills, yet, film after film went to his classmate from FTII, Rajesh Khanna.

'It was a string of failures, but I didn't doubt my capability. I knew I had to learn more. I learned I had to make contacts, and be with people. I could not be alone. I went door to door with my portfolio. One producer told me to tear off my diploma. "Actors are not trained, they are born," he said.'

'I was born also, trained also. What is your problem?' Ghai wanted to ask the producer.

He was twenty one at the time, and finally so close to realizing the dreams he had prepared for almost a lifetime. By then, perhaps, acting had become larger than a dream, an ambition. It was his love.

Umair Haque, Director of Havas Media Labs and author of *Betterness: Economics for Humans* and *The New Capitalist Manifesto: Building a Disruptively Better Business*, wrote in a Harvard Business Review blog post in October, 2012 on love and finding purpose in life. 'Be uncool enough to love. Purpose is a kind of love; it bridges the gap between the individual and the world. Yet, at every turn, in our brain-dead cult of the glacial machine, we're discouraged from even using the word love—unless, of course, when it serves the consumerist purpose of selling diamonds or cheese burgers or SUVs. So we substitute lower-quality ingredients for it, talking about "passion" or "dreams" or "bucket lists".'

'Purpose is love, not just little-l love, but Big Love, the grand affair that defines a life—first between you and your better, fuller, truer, worthier self; and then between your self and the world. And the longer you spend insulated in the armor of ironic detachment, icy cool in your igloo—the longer you're on something like a permanent vacation in the lifeless arctic wastelands of the empty tundras of the human soul.'

Ghai's love was big. Acting and films had bridged the gap between him and his worthier, truer self, and between him and the rest of the world. It was through acting he had understood the world he had come to love. It was his discovery of a whole new sky for himself, a whole new world.

'I was struggling for five years; I didn't want to go back to Delhi. I knew if I was talented it will work. I had to learn the environment of the industry. I asked people how the industry works. Assistant directors, producers became my teachers. I had to go drinking with them. That was a big struggle for me. I had never had alcohol before, and for me to start drinking was very difficult.'

What followed was a period of tribulation. Doors were literally shut or never opened for Ghai. He recalls a day when he went to a studio to meet a producer: 'The gatekeeper did not let me go in. I was asked who I do know in the studio. But I knew no one, and I was turned away.'

Always a loner, Ghai really had no friends, mentors, colleagues to speak of or speak to. His only recourse was inspirational books. 'I thought I am a failure; let me learn from these books. Those books helped me a lot.'

TAPPING YOUR FULL POTENTIAL

Ghai did finally manage to get a few roles as an actor, but then he realized that something he had been striving for was not something that would keep him engaged for long.

'Things were happening, not happening. But I realized that I was not enjoying it, I was restless.'

He knew he had to do something more, build on his talent, and fully harness his potential. 'When acting didn't work, I rediscovered myself. I got into writing. Sometimes we get into an ego trap and forget there are other avenues. Life will take you where you are best. You might try against your merits.'

He decided to put in all his energies into writing, and managed to sell six stories to a producer in one year. But all the six films flopped. Ghai had been out of FTII for five years now, between 1973-1977, and his first major breakthrough boomeranged.

'They took my story, but did not let me direct it. So I flopped as a writer. "Tumahari kahani to chalti nahi hai".'

One of Ghai's epochal hits, *Kalicharan*, was rejected many times, while his other stories were picked by producers. *Kalicharan* was even rejected by Ghai's friend, actor Shatrughan Sinha, for whom the story had been written. Ultimately veteran producer Ramesh Sippy liked the story and asked Ghai to direct the film.

OPPORTUNITY COMES WHEN YOU FEEL YOU ARE LEAST PREPARED FOR IT

But Ghai had trained as an actor and had no knowledge of editing or camera. 'I was a failure actor, and I didn't know how to operate a camera or the basics of editing. But I took the cameraman into confidence and learnt from him.'

Kalicharan was a defining film for Ghai. It was a huge hit and launched Ghai's career as a director. However, in entertainment, much like in sports, success comes and goes with the blink of an eye.

'After two hits, my film *Krodhi* flopped, and none of the stars wanted to work with me. One producer had signed me, but he said that he would only let me work with a star cast. If stars don't work with you, then it will be tough.'

'I asked him why a producer has to depend on stars, which means good stories don't work. I created a story where the leading stars were not required. I told him the story of *Vidhata*, which needed a retired, old actor, and a fresh, young face. The film had Dilip Kumar and launched Sanjay Dutt.'

The film *Vidhata* ran for seventy-five weeks, a failure had now morphed into a showman. Ghai delivered blockbuster after another, a string of films like *Karma*, *Saudagar*, *Khalnayak* that cemented his position as a director with a golden touch. And then the film *Trimurti* happened, audiences rejected it. The film flopped miserably and Ghai's abilities as a director were under question once again.

TREAT SUCCESS LIKE FAILURE

'I was serious after the failure of *Krodhi*. But after *Trimurti* I was really laughing. I decided to make a film on the life of a woman because I was getting typecast as an action director.'

Pardes followed, which again set the cash registers ringing. But Ghai was getting ready to move on.

'Mai bore ho gaya hits se,' he says. It was around that time he revisited the experiences of his student life, he met children from various parts of the country everyday who had the same dreams as he when he had first moved to Mumbai. He decided to build a state-of-the-art film school in Bollywood city. Directors and producers had built studios in Mumbai, but no institution on film education.

'When I started meeting children from various states, they would ask me for work and I would be reminded of my initial, struggle days. I would often ask myself, how do I know if he is talented or not. I wanted to open a unique kind of institute.'

This was a gargantuan project for any filmmaker. Ghai ignored the cynics and turned his passion into education. He turned his production house into a corporate company and raised money. Ghai is the first filmmaker to go corporate with a production house. Mukta Arts became a private limited company.

'After 100 years of cinema, someone had to open a film school in Bombay. I travelled all over the world, did full research on how to design a new syllabus, looking into the needs of the future. I did not surrender my education to NCERT and the University Grants Commission.'

Ghai had invested nearly twenty crore rupees, when things went awry with the government. After years, the government raised questions on the validity of the permissions granted to Ghai. 'I have got stuck but I have to survive.'

He has invested about Rs 80 crore in the project till now, his life's savings have gone into building Whistling Woods International. After a lifetime of achievements and accomplishments, Ghai is feeling far from fulfilled. He is anxious. 'In the end I am feeling the presence of failure, I had set aside my own film career for this. I couldn't focus. If things would have gone as planned, we would have valued the company at Rs 500 crore. But this incident has increased my understanding of life.'

'I still live in a 3-bhk (three bedroom, hall, kitchen) and I built a campus. People kept asking why did you do that; why did you spend all your money? Has any filmmaker built a film institute? Were they fools? You made so much money till *Taal*. After ten years the government wants to take it (Whistling Woods International) back. The court tells you it doesn't belong to you. But I know I will come back. I know one thing: Subhash Ghai will not die, without being what he wants to be.'

The showman is setting the stage for his comeback, even as he tries to stand up once again.

WHY I FAILED

- I aspired for the wrong things that would eventually fail to enthuse me
- I took time to realize my full potential
- I was utopian in my outlook as I invested my lifetime savings and energies into one project

Advice

- Build your inner strength
- There can be advantages even in disadvantageous situations
- Take time to learn from your failures
- Love what you do. Passion is not half as powerful as love

'Sometimes life does not happen the way you want it to'

AJIT GULABCHAND

Ajit Gulabchand, besides being known for his Bentley Phantom and his distinct style of dressing—usually spotted in a pair of blue jeans and a blazer—is near-synonymous with the most landmark infrastructure projects in India. The chairman and managing director of Hindustan Construction Company gave Mumbai its first Sea Link. HCC has also made it to the Guinness Book of World Records for building the longest barrage in the world—the Farakka barrage in West Bengal. Gulabchand's ambitious Lavasa project hit a road block, as the Ministry of Environment and Forests charged the company of environmental violations. Gulabchand is refreshingly honest as he speaks about his vulnerabilities and challenges in dealing with the Indian government.

The Difficulty Of Planning

Well, the world is an uncertain, swirling, confusing place. To be able to survive it and fight it, we need multiple plans. If Plan A fails, there should be an equally good plan to fall back on. But how often do we plan for failure? Mostly, never. We usually work with the assumption that our Plan A, possibly our best, would work. Planning can get particularly challenging when there are several variables involved.

Uncertainty takes on a new dimension, a new meaning, a new breadth in India. Businesses here work with and around constant policy flip-flops, a vulnerable economic environment and reams of bureaucracy and red tape. Dealing with uncertainty in India can leave the most battle-scarred businessmen befuddled, and Ajit Glulabchand has been one of them.

The chairman and managing director of one of India's largest infrastructure companies, the Hindustan Construction Company, failed in putting together an alternative to his Plan A, when he envisioned a city that would introduce India to a new way of living. Lavasa, the marquee development project of Hindustan Construction Company (HCC), was introduced to the world in quintessential Gulabchand-like grandeur and style, with full page ads in leading dailies across the country.

For Gulabchand, building Lavasa was a pioneering move of a lifetime. He was treading into a territory which had largely been a government domain. How many industrialists have come forward to build a city from scratch? There are massive investments and risks involved. Getting all stakeholders on board, permissions, and funds makes it a very challenging exercise for even the most seasoned. The 'hill station legislation' passed by the Maharashtra government cleared the way for Lavasa.

Gulabchand's planning was precise to the last detail—he even discussed the variety of saplings to be planted which would be best suited for Lavasa climes and would not only replenish the water table but also increase it. All permissions for construction were taken. Tens of thousands of workers had migrated from different states and cities to build what was to be a city which would redefine living in India.

Lavasa was to be built over three stages. Work was on in full swing; the local school was operational, teaching around hundreds of children of labuorers who were working on the site. Spread across twenty five thousand acres, several investors across the country had bought into Gulabchand's dream. Around fifty thousand crore were to be invested in the project, and nearly four thousand crore had been invested by Lavasa upto 2010. Two thousand people had bought homes in Lavasa city. Gulbachand showcased what could be India's urban planning marvel on international platforms and went about setting the stage for the Initial Public Offering of Lavasa Corporation. The company had plans of coming out with a public offer by December, 2010. The size of the public offer was to be two thousand crore rupees.

With several stakeholders involved, money was being pumped into the project, the best of design teams were called, and owning a part of Lavasa was fast becoming an aspirational dream for many. The stakes were high. But then great accomplishments involve greater risks, and Gulabchand, with decades of experience of working with the government, was no rookie in dealing with risks.

Gulabchand had factored in almost every risk. What he failed at anticipating was the implications of contrary decisions of the State government and the Central government. There are certain things that you don't take for granted in a country in transition. And perhaps uniformity in policymaking and consistency in decision making is what Gulabchand had taken for granted.

While all environmental clearances from the Maharashtra government were in place, the Central government did a summersault which brought the hill city to a halt.

The Maharashtra government took seven years to give permissions, as a hundred-year-old-group, 'We couldn't have screwed up that badly,' says Gulabchand.

The Union Ministry of Environment and Forests (MoEF) issued a show cause notice to Lavasa Corporation Limited for violating environmental laws in November, 2010. Subsequently, the State government directed the Maharashtara Pollution Control Board to file criminal proceedings against the promoters. It was the first such infrastructure/construction project where a criminal proceeding had been initiated.

While Gulabchand focussed on building his vision, he failed at anticipating the worse that could happen in an emerging economy which is mired in policy uncertainty. He took on debt, heavily leveraged himself, and placed all his bets on Lavasa. HCC went into an over two hundred crore rupee debt in 2011–12, after posting a profit of seventy one crore rupees the previous year. Too much passion can be dangerous in any situation, and business is no different. When we tend to be consumed by an idea, a plan, a project, we start breathing it, living it, and our capability to fathom grave negativity about it dithers and fades away.

Gulabchand was in Paris finalizing a deal with Areva when he heard about the notice from the environment ministry that ordered HCC to stop all construction work and break down all that had been built so far. The news did not come through a notice but through a press conference beamed live across news channels. The notice reached the HCC headquarters later in the evening that day. All employees, stakeholders were in a state of shock. Gulabchand was about two weeks away from Lavasa's Initial Public Offering, which has now been put on hold.

Gulabchand, a veteran in fighting battles, had not anticipated that Lavasa could put the fortunes of the entire group on a cliff.

'If you think that's the right thing to do, you will meet obstacles where people will not understand; some will deliberately create obstacles. You know you have to fight and move on. You have to have the humility to comprehend that there will be things beyond your control. You can't fight blindly. You can't hit out like a wounded animal. You will not win. If you really want to do something pathbreaking, there will be obstacles. You have to get around them and strategize.'

BOLDNESS HAS GENIUS, POWER, MAGIC IN IT

He had, for long, gotten himself out of difficult situations, always maneuvered and strategized a way out. There had been setbacks and Ajit Gulabchand did usually opt for the challenging, the difficult, and emerged stronger.

In 1983, when Gulabchand had assumed charge as managing director of Hindustan Construction Company, a tussle was already on within the Walchand Hirachand family. After over a decade long battle, he took over as chairman and managing director in 1994. HCC was the black sheep of the group, making only about five crore rupees as profit. Gulabchand has built HCC into one of the most influential business empires in the country. He took on the daunting challenge to give Mumbai its first Sea Link. The Bandra-Worli project took nearly a decade to complete. An engineering feat, the Sea Link is yet to break even. There are six hundred crore worth of claims still being discussed. Meanwhile, HCC's market capitalization has dipped to a near-fifth of its value from two years ago. Lavasa has bogged down the group beyond the expectations of many.

'The real charge was that we should have taken the Central government's permission and not the State's. We were very clear we don't need that permission for the first two thousand hectares. Finally the PM (Manmohan Singh) intervened, and Jairam Ramesh (former Environment Minister) backed down,' says an animated Gulabchand.

As the fate of the group he had built painstakingly nearly over eighteen years hung in limbo, Gulabchand was quick enough to strategize a fight back strategy. 'When I filed my case against the Environment Ministry, I also filed a personal malafide case against Jairam Ramesh (the then Environment Minister—May 2009–July 2011). I fought legally and politically. Some people said: Why don't you negotiate? But I wanted to fight it out.'

'The Maharashtra government was in a quandary. Jairam Ramesh kept saying the orders have come from above. I knew one needed patience, because this is the way things happen. Courts take long. Everything takes long. It's the reality and you have to live with it.'

Gulabchand's initial reaction was of denial: 'I thought this cannot happen. But we realized very quickly it had. We moved court over the weekend. Livelihoods were at stake. IPO was around the corner. You have to understand the nature of the attack. In a free country, there is supposed to be rule-of-law. When the process is not followed, then you know there is a motivation behind it. When you realize something is wrong, you get the moral courage to fight it. I studied this man (Jairam Ramesh), because I couldn't afford to make a mistake. We fought him on every media. The more we exposed, there was a lot of sympathy. When the war begins, then the war becomes your target.'

Gulabchand went about aggressively restructuring the debt. In a first quarter (FY 2012-13) press release, the company declared that restructuring of its thirty-two hundred crore debt had been approved, and that timely restructuring would improve cash flow and provide room for operating during the challenging period.

'Sometimes it helps to get into a new platform. You realize that there were many who did not know—like the PM (Prime Minister Manmohan Singh) did not know. We also felt we needed to educate more people. We communicated with the villagers, who stood by us, and that also tells us that we are doing something right. We found people supporting us in the government. Until one is committed, there is hesitancy. As Goethe has said: "Whatever you can do or dream you can, begin it. Boldness has genius, power, and magic in it".'

It has been these words that have guided Gulabchand's philosophy towards life. He continues to dream, of bringing Lavasa's IPO back, of building a world class city (the multi-crore hill city project got the clearance from the Environment Ministry in November, 2011), of bringing debt down to manageable levels, of further strengthening the company's order-book, of building more highways, and of being a world-class infrastructure company.

Lavasa is delayed by nearly three years. Business partnerships have fallen out, and there is a huge opportunity cost involved. But Gulabchand knows he will be able to pull it all together, once again.

And this time he will be smarter than before. But there is a question that comes up intermittently through his conversation: 'Why isn't anybody shocked that this can happen in a democratic country?'

WHY I FAILED

- Heavily leveraged myself for a high risk project
- My enthusiasm and optimism clouded my skeptical mind

Advice

- Whatever you can do or dream you can, begin it. Boldness has genius, power, and magic in it

- If you think that's the right thing to do, you will meet obstacles where people will not understand, and some will deliberately create obstacles

- Have the humility to comprehend that there will be things beyond your control

'If people are given a chance they can perform miracles'

SMINU JINDAL

Sminu Jindal is the only business person in the country to run a multi-million dollar business from a wheelchair. It was through her sheer determination, grit and brilliance that she broke into the traditional male bastion of iron and steel. Jindal has been at the forefront of driving growth and innovation at Jindal Saw, one of the flagship companies of OP Jindal group. It has been under Sminu's leadership that the company has diversified from pipes to infrastructure, logistics, transportation. Sminu is also passionately involved in creating public spaces for people with reduced mobility.

'I can fight the alligator', she said, and the engineer who wanted to wrestle the alligator in an expandor at a Jindal SAW plant in Texas, US, gave her a scornful look. Within minutes, Sminu Jindal, the managing director of Jindal Saw, was rattling off reasons why the alligator was in there to the engineer—'Welding is not right, you are using too much oxygen,' she said. 'Control the flame.' A while later, the engineer who wanted to wrestle the alligator, came back and said, 'Sminu you are right.' She recalls, years later, sitting in her elegant and understated office in the heart of New Delhi.

The alligator story is particularly fascinating in Sminu Jindal's life. It is a sort of a metaphor for her belief in self and the scorns and jibes that were thrown at her as she went about proving to her family and the world outside that a half-paralysed woman could indeed run a business successfully. For the lack of a better definition, Sminu's failure could be characterized as a social failure.

I use the term 'social' because Sminu's failures were largely associated with fighting perception battles within the society. How you define failure is important, because the type of failure will determine what you take away from it and how you counter it. Failure means different things for different people. What might be a failure for you could be inconsequential for someone else. It is a bit like clay, it moulds and remoulds. There are some who strategize their own failure, there are others who fail because of a miscalculated decisions or actions, and then there are those who are set up for failure. Sminu Jindal was set up for failure when she met with an accident at the age of eleven and was paralysed from waist down. Jindal has been fighting alligators since.

How many of us have really wrestled alligators? Metaphorically speaking, of course. Alligators are gargantuan reptiles and most often those who fight them are considered foolish.

In our world, I consider alligators as daunting challenges that we very rarely find the courage to take on, primarily because we are often sure of failing the fight. The fear of loss and defeat paralyses us into inaction, and it is in that act of inaction—I would like to attribute 'inaction' as an act, because that too is a conscious choice that we make—that we try and find our comfort, excuses, solace. We tend to reassure ourselves that we did do what we thought was best. But did we, really? Or, did we just take the easier way out? Not fighting the alligators would be the easier thing to do. But then, until we have fought them, we wouldn't know if we have failed or succeeded at fighting them.

Sminu Jindal's alligators, however, are unique. She had to fight a physical disability and perceptions that came with being a physically handicapped and a woman.

'Many would say, losing your mobility at the age of eleven is a setback enough to set you up for failure in life,' she says.

NOBODY SAID IT WILL BE EASY

An ordinarily willed person could have taken the physical handicap as a life-defining failing. But Sminu Jindal, instead, armed herself with knowledge and confidence as she went about traversing life.

Born into the fourth largest industrial house in India, the OP Jindal Group, Sminu Jindal took on challenging roles and projects and turned around adverse business situations to prove her business mettle.

'It's probably easier to deal with a physical handicap when one is born with it,' she says.

A physical disability can be debilitating not only physically, but emotionally and psychologically as well. It can crush your confidence to the extent that you might not be able to ever regain it.

There were no examples for her to follow. No patterns or lessons. She has had to set her own path and chalk her own destiny. Today, she leads Jindal Saw from a wheelchair. Paralyzed from waist down, she broke into what are considered the traditional male bastion sectors of infrastructure, logistics, transportation, and steel.

'I started my career with a challenge. I was the only women in my entire family who got into iron and steel. People would be surprised at my choice; I would tell them I don't have to lift it, I just have to manage people. People make your company.'

Every stage, age, and phase was fraught with different challenges. She cried, fought, tried, and conquered. She remembers having cried herself to sleep many nights when she had to give up dancing, something she loved, after the accident. Or the time when she could no longer be a child like other children.

'Whenever you have conquered one setback, there is another one. Being a woman and being on a wheelchair does work against you. But then you look at life half-empty or half-full. And I look at my life half-full,' she says.

So, is she the eternal optimist who is able to conquer her darkest thoughts?

'No,' she says. 'But I am able to ride over my low phases. I can see the light and work towards it with perseverance. If you have the desire, God shows you the way.'

She is the first woman from her family to enter the business, the only business leader in India who is physically handicapped and wheels herself on work sites and to conferences and meetings across the world.

How She Does It

She takes her disability in her stride. She accepted early on in life that her challenges and battles would be different. Not only was she a woman, but a woman who needed physical assistance at every step.

She learned, she says, that she still had her arms, and that she could still employ her brains and her heart. Over the years as a business leader in a country which is still patriarchal, where women are not necessarily the first choice to lead a family-run business, Sminu Jindal is an anomaly. She has managed to turn around every sick unit she was assigned. And every project she was assigned has been a make- or break-Sminu opportunity.

She dreamt of being a business person since she was a child and she has pursued her dream of being a business leader with dogged focus, perseverance, discipline, and conviction.

She was nineteen when she was assigned what was considered a near impossible task of literally reinventing a foil unit under the flagship OP Jindal Group. The ultra-thin stainless steel foil manufacturing unit was on the verge of shutting down. And that was Sminu's first turnaround opportunity. She was categorically told to either turn it around or step back.

Sminu had multiple challenges to deal with here—make a sick unit profitable (many had tried and failed); get employees who had been working for OP Jindal, her grandfather, to work for her; and challenge old practices and processes that had been followed for years.

This was the first test of her ambition, ability, and drive to establish herself in corporate India. And Sminu Jindal took on the challenge of turning around Swastik Foils head-on. She went about rallying support, turning pessimism into optimism, inspiring confidence, and taking the right business decisions.

Her actions displayed conviction, belief, and confidence in herself. She did not turn away from taking unpopular decisions. If she was convinced, she would make every effort to convince those who weren't. She came in like a storm shaking conventions, beliefs, and stereotypes.

She challenged the old way of doing things. She brought financial discipline, bottom line efficiency, and back to basics focus on the company. She realized rather quickly that the company was wasting time and resources in beating the foil extra thin, because it couldn't really get any thinner than what it already was. Much like what the Starbucks coffee retail chain founder, Howard Schultz, did when Starbucks was running into huge losses and he was brought back on the board to turn it around. Schultz realized that the company was literally washing millions down the sink, so he installed a serrated internal ring inside a pitcher to guide how much milk a barista should use for a latte. A small but a very significant decision to put in a process that stopped wastage of milk helped Starbucks save millions of dollars.

What Sminu proposed was unthinkable to those working with the company for years. It was what the company had stood for, and reassessing the company's USP was never part of the plan. Though she was undeterred and confident that her assessment was accurate, she knew her confidence alone was not enough. She had to inspire confidence in her team.

Her greatest challenge was to convince those who had much more experience in the industry, had been with the group since she was a child, and believed that they understood the business much better. Sminu's conviction led to many exits from the company; a close aide of her grandfather walked out in a huff; many who stayed back doubted Sminu's capabilities, and cringed at her guts. But Sminu Jindal proved it to herself and others that she had the sound instincts of running a successful business—a point she would have to prove often.

'My only contribution was that you cannot make extra thin foil. If people are given a chance they can perform miracles,' she says, decades after her first successful turnaround story.

The stainless steel unit was her first turnaround story, many more followed later. Years later, when Sminu had clearly established herself, she was faced with the daunting task of turning around a sick unit in the US. 'The plant was massive; it could be seen on the map of Texas.'

The plant was one of the largest loss-making units of the group. Its losses could have taken down one of group's flagship companies, SAW Pipes. Sminu spent months at the plant, wheeling herself through the narrow corridors, working tirelessly from a cubby-hole cabin. Things were so bad that it got to a point when the unit didn't have money to pay for electricity for two days. It took Sminu six years to make the unit profitable. The plant went through an overhaul—once again Sminu took unpopular decisions, replaced people, change the technology, and worked on massive perception management strategy.

It was six years of sweat and toil, but that did not stop her from getting rid of the unit as soon as she had turned it around.

'It was like having a baby, but having less emotional attachment is very important,' she says.

Sminu was confident that capitalizing on opportunities in India would be a far more profitable for the business. She refocussed her energies back home, and went ahead with building Jindal Saw which has further diversified into businesses launched under its subsidiary, Jindal ITF, focussed on infrastructure (water, waste water, and solid waste management), transportation, and fabrication (high volume shipyards and rail wagons).

In the year 2000, Jindal SAW was a three hundred crore rupees company. The phenomenal growth to an over seven thousand crore rupees company has meant enormous hard work, 16-18 hour work days, and plant visits nearly everyday.' I love machines, love nuts and bolts; 'I love being at the plant. In summers I can stand around a furnace in a plant and not feel a thing. It's fun; it's poetry to watch a machine move.'

'There is so much to do, so how can one waste a life feeling sad and sorry? Affect a few lives, if not many. Leave something behind.'

WHY I FAILED

- Being a woman on a wheelchair had set me up for failure

Advice

- Be attached to people, not entities
- Focus on strengths and capitalize on them
- Believe in yourself, because if you don't, no one will

*'We are not active planners of
our own fate'*

WILLIAM BISSELL

William Bissell has gone on to prove again and again that capitalism can go hand-in-hand with socialism. He is the pioneer of the concept of community-owned companies in India. The man who made going 'desi' cool, Bissell introduced middle class India to the various hues and textures of Indian textiles. His is a fascinating journey of self discovery, as he went about weaving one of the most unique brands in the country—Fabindia.

FAILURE IS INEVITABLE

When you want to be a pioneer, to do what others haven't, to create what most can only talk about, and to see an opportunity where others see obstacles, then failure is inevitable. That's the spirit pioneers embed in their lives. They work very hard, sacrifice, take risks, and when they fail, they rise again. Pioneers have a way of often making their success look effortless. William Bissell, managing director of Fabindia, India's largest community-owned company, has that ability of keeping the affects of both success and failure at arms length. He doesn't let either slow him down.

In 2004, when he failed to raise funds for the company he had spent more than fifteen years nurturing (Fabindia), he was disappointed and down for a day or two—but soon after he was ready to keep going and he used the lessons from failure to better the business model and further build on the company's supply chain.

'We like to think we are active planners of our own fate, but we are not. However, you can be an active planner of improving your quality. Because we are so deeply conditioned in thinking of external factors affecting our performance—it absolves us of having to look at our role. That is the hardest to do.'

Bissell is the first business person to have perfected a community-owned business model in India. When Bissell approached investors for funding—Fabindia had become synonymous with everything Indian, ethnic, and chic. The company had grown exponentially and had stores in cities and towns across the country; profits and money had been made for all involved, including the artisans. For the very first time, craftsmen owned the company for which they worked. He had brought India's forgotten weaves and textiles to the middle-class.

Bissell is the force behind two pioneering ideas: the community owned company model, and organized retail. Both concepts were virtually non-existent at the time. Nobody seemed to doubt Bissell's vision or intent, and yet he had failed to convince potential investors of the company's profitability.

With clinical precision, he analysed his failure. Pioneers are usually not the sorts to take failure personally, and he didn't either. He was aware of the market conditions and the unforgiving nature of retail, and he knew that his supply chain still needed to be perfected.

Building a reliable network of suppliers has only been one of the formidable challenges. Higher real estate costs, poor infrastructure, tremendous cost and margin pressures and no ecosystem whatsoever for scale were some other issues plaguing retail.

'You have to play a very sharp game. There are tremendous cost and margin pressures, within that environment. The advent of retailers who are ready to take significant losses makes it all the more challenging—you have pressures from all sides. You have to manage them. We have a lot of hidden constraints. When I started out there was no ecosystem,' says Bissell.

Three years later, Bissell found a backer. Former World Bank President James Wolfensohn's private investment fund picked up a six percent stake for $11 million, which took Fabindia's valuation to around seven hundred and fifty crore rupees. But Bissell's response to success is as matter-of-fact as his earlier failure to raise funds was. He almost gives credit to India's economic environment: 'We raised money in 2007 at a very good valuation. The India story was very hot at the time.'

Perhaps it is also this ability of not taking success or failure too seriously that enables a person to be a pioneer. Bissell steps back and gauges each situation with brutal objectivity. He will slice a positive or a negative development neatly to analyze the how's and why's.

'I come from a rather privileged background; my challenges weren't as daunting as that of a first generation entrepreneur—entrepreneurs who have created out of nothing.'

Bissell has taken every setback as an opportunity to evaluate and improve. It was after he failed to raise funds in 2004 that he decided to work on his book, *Making India Work*. The book is a diagnosis of what ails India; Bissell suggests solutions based on his own experiences. At around the same time that Bissell was working on the book, there was peer pressure on him to be seen and heard at events and networking parties.

'I couldn't join because I was busy doing so many things. I spent that time in writing a book, I really focused on the book. Spent my time and energy on the book, and the two people I wanted to meet, read the book and came to me. The world becomes different as you develop your faculties.'

'If you develop yourself, the world becomes deeper,' he says.

'The world is like an onion. You slice it at different levels, and where you are is how you slice it.'

DON'T MULL OR OVERANALYSE. JUST MOVE!

When William Bissell, a graduate in government policy took over a small handloom-focused export house and decided to scale it up into a nation-wide retail chain, with artisans as shareholders, it was considered a bizarre, outlandish, and near-impossible business to do. Back in the nineties, the concept of community-owned companies was as new as liberalization. Artisans could work for you, but they could not own the company. Not only was Bissell working out an entirely new business model, but he was also beginning to work in organized retail, a business fraught with ambiguity and risks. Bissell did not have a rule book to which he could refer. It has been, he says, a relentless process of discovery.

However, in many ways, Bissell is fairly nonchalant about the trials and tribulations of being a pioneer. You shouldn't dwell, or overanalyse, as you continue to move with focus and determination, he says. 'Discouragement does not stick around. I tend to get down, for a day or two. And then I bounce back. I don't dwell on discouragement. When you obsess and stress about it, it acquires a much bigger dimension.'

Bissell took over an export house started by his father John Bissell. Fabindia was specifically set up with the goal of promoting handlooms of India. It was founded in 1960 and initially run from the two rooms in John Bissell's New Delhi home.

When William took over in 1999, there were many who questioned his approach. He capitalized on his innate sense for retail, which he says is his second skin, and gave the customers what they wanted, even as he kept the socialistic vision of the brand and company intact. Making profits and fighting for workers' welfare don't necessarily go together, but William has established a strong case of 'conscious capitalism'—an antithesis to crony capitalism that has come to plague India and Indian businesses.

Today, Fabindia is one of most profitable retailers in the country. Fabindia has over twenty-two thousand artisans working with it. They are all shareholders through an elaborate community-owned model which William has evolved over the years.

The first resistance to be part of the community model came from the artisans themselves, Bissell went from village to village explaining the concept of shareholding and ownership to craftsmen who often had no concept of a regular income and had little pride for their craft.

'A lot of people said, "aap kagaz ka tukda de rahe hai (you are just giving us a piece of paper)". They didn't know that the piece of paper gave them rights, dividend. There was a lot of frustration on the way: there were disappointments and challenges. But if I am convinced, I plough along. I was at a point where I knew this is a model that works.'

In the last decade, Fabindia has grown from one store in New Delhi to a network of a hundred and sixty-nine stores across the country and eight stores abroad. There is a dedicated supply chain organization with eighty-six thousand artisans working through community-owned companies. Fabindia outsources all the manufacturing of its merchandize to these community-owned companies. In India, where comprehending the dynamics of retail is tougher than understanding the workings of the government, Bissell has cracked the code—of relentlessly pursuing profits with a social goal.

William has built the institution from ground-up. He devised the concept of community owned companies (COCs) in 2007 in order to strengthen the supply chain for Fabindia's aggressive retail expansion plans.

Apart from developing the supply chain, Fabindia is also strengthening the technological know-how and improving the quality standards of the supply chain. A designers' panel works closely with artisans to design products that are marketable. Artisans are constantly drilled with the nuances of retail—the importance of meeting quality, design standards, and deadlines. In fact, persons heading production centres are required to undertake a MBA course conducted in association with the International Management School, Delhi.

Bissell's vision plan is now to move to tier-two cities. Bringing in more investors is inevitable, but he will work hard to try and balance investor expectations and artisans' aspirations.

Until now, business has been a means to alleviate poverty and empowering lives. He has delivered. Because he has been discerning while picking his investors. He has ensured that they share his vision as much as they want a share in the profits.

Bissell says that years of aimless wandering has aided his ability to think clearly and with focus. Yes, aimless wandering seems purposeless, but it's an essential fuel for the creative mind. And Bissell's second trick is daydreaming. 'This [daydreaming] should constitute 20 percent of your day,' he says.

'When you do aimless wandering, it opens your mind to all kind of different things. Daydreaming is the ultimate exercise of the mind. Through fantasies come the most fantastic ideas. I have aimlessly wandered so much.'

'I have done something I have cared deeply about. I meet people who ask me to give them an idea which makes them a lot of money. You have to have a passion. Find out what are you passionate about. Money cannot be a passion. My passion lies in developing a model that makes artisans, craftpersons, and producers a part of the opportunities created by thriving markets and organized retail.

WHY I FAILED

- My business model needed sharper focus

Advice

- Wander aimlessly—aimless wandering opens your mind
- Through fantasies come the most fantastic ideas
- Don't dwell on failures. The more you mull, the larger they will appear

'*You realize you are alone. Your fight is your fight. Your battle is your battle*'

SANJIV GOENKA

Sanjiv Goenka, the vice chairman of RPG Enterprises, has never believed in taking the easier route to success—whether it was his acquisition of power giant CESC, or of Firstsource Solutions—he has always managed to silence the skeptics through his acute business sense. Goenka knows a good business opportunity when he sees one—the group also runs Saregama India Ltd and retail chain Spencer Retail, among other businesses.

OH, THAT IDEALISM

Even if you are the scion of one of the oldest business families in India, the heir to a multi-thousand crore business literally built over nearly two centuries, have had the privilege and opportunity to learn from the best, your journey to the very top could still be fraught with challenges, fractiousness, and loneliness. Sanjiv Goenka's journey has been somewhat like that. Born into privilege and in the lap of opportunity, Goenka often found himself often alone while battling the most crucial, life-altering circumstances.

It had been nearly a decade after he had worked Calcutta Electricity Supply Corporation (CESC) to life—a company he had bought much to the apprehension of everyone, including his father, the late Mr R.P. Goenka, who continues to be his inspiration today. Goenka was all of twenty eight, brimming with enthusiasm, idealism, and the belief that he could bring change when he decided to buy out the ailing CESC which, at the time, was infamous for nasty power cuts that would last 12 to 14 hours in Calcutta (Now Kolkata). It was a company with massive transmission and distribution losses (nearly 28 percent), insignificant profits (five crore rupees) and machines that were running at half the capacity.

'When this proposal came to me, something told me it's a great opportunity. When I spoke to my father about CESC, he said: "Roz bijli jaayegi aur saara sheher tumhe gaali dega" (the entire city will curse you whenever there is a power cut).' His father, the founder of RPG group, the late Dr Rama Prasad Goenka, was as sceptical about his younger son's foray into power generation as everyone else. Sanjiv Goenka walked into the office of CESC after the acquisition, only to be greeted by a funeral pyre and an effigy which said 'Sanjiv Goenka murdabaad'.

A prayer ceremony is usually conducted to invoke blessings as part of a traditional custom that is followed in India on the start of any new project or a new beginning. Goenka sat alone at the ceremony, as his colleagues in CESC boycotted him and his decision. 'There was not even one person who came for the puja. There was a lot of hostility.'

Perhaps it was the experience, the learnings from nurturing CESC, of convincing every employee that he had a vision for the company—he had managed to turn the hostile team into one that would stand by him in his darkest hour—that prepared Goenka for another challenge which would pit him against government and his own industry colleagues a decade later.

Fear of failure often deters us from taking that first step, from even trying, from listening to that inner voice that says: Yes, I can do it. 'I knew I shouldn't fail for the lack of trying. I would rather try and fail than not even try and de-facto fail,' says Goenka.

Within years, CESC had been turned around, a company that had been written off emerged as serious competition, debt had reduced significantly, and efficiencies increased. 'Bit by bit, everything started falling into place,' says Goenka.

Goenka managed the unions, and trimmed the workforce by thirty-five hundred people in a single day without anyone protesting. The plant load factor at CESC power stations has nearly doubled since and debt to equity ratio is the lowest it has ever been. 'It was about being completely transparent with the team, about engaging with each of them and telling them I am not here to take your job. What they saw in me was sincerity and hope,' he adds.

Ironically, CESC's competition was also its principal supplier and regulator. As CESC started competing, the principal supplier and competitor started restricting supplies, permissions for capacity addition were withheld, and the company was not allowed to take business decisions such as increasing tariffs. It was 1999 when Goenka decided to go to the Kolkata high court against the administration.

Goenka had successfully managed to keep the fear of failure and emotional pressures aside (his father didn't eat food for two days) and had taken that leap of faith when he acquired CESC—he once again voluntarily got into choppy waters. However, this time, the enthusiasm and idealism of youth was behind him, and he was a seasoned business person, a heavyweight in his own right.

That was perhaps the first time that an industrialist had decided to take the government to court and Goenka, once again, found himself all alone. 'Jal mai rehkar magar se bair nahin hota (when you live in water, you don't make enemies with a crocodile),' is what he was told often.

'Strangely the entire industrial community of Bengal was rallying against me. I was feeling challenged from all quarters, fighting the state government and fifty corporates.'

Goenka had withstood and overcome a similar situation a decade back when he bought CESC, but this Sanjiv Goenka who was challenging the state government a decade later was far more confident, with greater conviction and a depth of experience that only comes with nurturing a company back to life with indefatigable focus and determination. Goenka had rallied support and turned a hostile team into a support bank that he would rely on in his hour of need and crisis, and with his business sense, administration, and leadership had altered the destinies of thousands of employees associated with the company.

Moment Of Truth

His success came with many new friends, but his failures and vulnerability also isolated him, most importantly, from within his family.

As Goenka fought the legal battle, the company was once again on the brink of bankruptcy and there was no help (financial or emotional) coming from anywhere.

'The family refused to fund CESC; I didn't know how I would pay salaries,' he says.

'There was but a mirage of support. The essence of a joint family is that there are different cogs and then you make a wheel, and then you realize that you are the cogs and the wheel,' he adds.

In most situations, help does come from the most unexpected quarters. As Goenka went through a 'very emotionally stressful period', he approached ICICI bank for help and managed to convince the then CEO, K.V. Kamath, of his vision for the company.

'ICICI bank came forward, and as I was going through the process, I realized you are alone in your battles. The realization is not a good realization. It is a moment of truth that took some time for me to overcome. You realize that the support system you had always counted on is only semantically there, but not really there. The only people who were there for me were my father, wife, and children.'

Goenka did not get deterred by the negativity. It was emotionally exhausting, but the realization also motivated him. He wanted to prove it to himself and everyone around him, those who had doubted him that he could achieve the goal he had set out for.

I kept the negativity aside. I focussed on the job, and when you are coming to terms with reality, you realize that support never existed. Whenever there has been a crisis, you will realize that you have battled it alone.'

Goenka won the high court case. 'Once we won the high court case, then there was no looking back. There was suddenly a lot of confidence in me as a leader,' he says.

'I have never been fazed by hostility,' he adds.

BUSINESS OF BURNING EFFIGIES, HOSTILITY, AND ISOLATION

For Goenka to witness a burning effigy of himself was unnerving, but it also strengthened his resolve to succeed.

As ironical as it may seem, Goenka's journey has been about proving himself constantly; as he achieved a milestone and proved the naysayers wrong, another battle, another milestone was set before him to achieve. In most cases, he had the choice to take the easy way out—he needn't have taken on the challenge of CESC and set himself up for failure, but it was for precisely that reason that he did. He knew the lessons in the process would be immeasurable, and they have been.

He need not have taken on the administration and fought a lone battle against the State government, but for him, it was a matter of redefining the way business was done in India. It was about a vision, a leadership thought. And most often, such pioneering journeys are made alone.

'It has been a tumultuous and satisfying journey. The city (Kolkata) has started having confidence in me. If I am doing something, it will be correct. This expectation is a scary thing; it has literally taken me forever to build such expectations of me.'

Goenka has been as driven by intuition and gut as by data and facts. His approach has been inclusive and of achieving consensus. But while decision making has been democratic, he has always been mindful of the fact that ultimately the buck stops at him—'That investors are there because of you.'

'My entire experience has made me a very self-assured person. A very secure person.'

'I am pretty clear on what I want to do and how to do it.'

'Today we are the best performing utility in India, and it is the same old team. My biggest achievement has been to motivate my team to deliver. We are now focussing on best practices and operational excellence. There was no reaction from the city when we increased tariffs. The city has started to have confidence that if Sanjiv Goenka is doing it, it will be correct. This expectation is a scary thing, but it keeps me engaged.'

WHY I FAILED

- I failed in my expectations of myself and of those around me. There was just a mirage of support around me

Advice

- Setting yourself up for failure can be an immensely learning experience
- Life's most challenging situations can bring out the best in you
- You are often loneliest in your most difficult situations
- Keep the negativity aside and focus on the job

'It was a Perfect Storm'

SHANKAR SHARMA

Shankar Sharma, the suave, articulate, brash, brave man of the Indian stock markets, is the founder of securities firm, First Global. Sharma fearlessly fought a bitter and brutal battle with the Indian government for three years. First Global is the first Indian company to be admitted to membership of the London Stock Exchange. Sharma continues to be the big bear of the Indian stock markets known for his contrarian calls. Currently, Sharma is putting in all his energies into his new venture Cerebra Brain Tech Pvt. Ltd—a research-based venture that seeks to provide solutions for neurological disorders like autism. His other passion is writing mystery novels and he is known to be unabashedly in love with his wife and business partner, Devina Mehra.

'Death was preferable at that point in time,' laments Shankar Sharma, founder of First Global.

Shankar Sharma's story is a classic story of liberalized India—there is phenomenal ambition, success, and opportunity, some of it because of the government and most of it despite the government.

A small town, middle-class boy strikes big in the Indian stock market, largely dominated by the cozy clubs and coteries, with hard work, intelligence, and sheer determination. He was an outsider in the equity markets until he grew on to become the big bear of the stock market and one of the highest taxpayers in India. That was at the start of the millennium, the year 2000. Sharma's tax payout at the time was larger than what most Bollywood stars paid in 2011-12.

His brokerage firm, First Global, became the first Indian company to be admitted to membership of the London Stock Exchange. It was rated among the three top brokerage houses in India by *Asia Money* magazine. The trading turnover of the First Global Group in the year 1999-2000 was seven thousand three hundred and forty-two crore.

It had been a dizzy, dream-like run for Shankar Sharma and his wife Devina Mehra who started the company together after Sharma quit his job with Citibank. Graduates of the Indian Institute of Management (IIM), they were the first in the family to turn entrepreneurs.

Until one day when one wrong investment decision put everything they had owned and built at stake.

It was in the summer of 2001. Sharma was travelling with his wife Devina Mehra, also partner in the firm to the US.

They had flown to New York for their NASDAQ accreditation interviews, when he got a call from the enforcement agency to report back to India as soon as possible.

Sharma and Devina landed in Mumbai at four in the morning, and went straight to their home in Colaba which had been sealed by the Income Tax Department. They had to spend the night in a hotel. Next morning, the Income Tax authorities opened the apartment and literally invaded it—its officers unceremoniously went through their cupboards, books, papers, photographs, letters; everything was pulled out, torn open, and violated on the pretext of finding undeclared/hidden income. 'A façade', says Sharma, as it would increasingly became apparent that a case was trying to be built against Sharma for his investment in a news portal, Tehelka.

Sharma was later told that he was being investigated for an alleged charge that he was part of the bear cartel responsible for the post-budget (stock market) crash in 2001.

Sharma's investment in Tehelka changed their life forever. It's an investment decision he continues to regret. The decision cost them everything they had built—their credibility was at stake and they were left penniless. Their bank accounts were frozen. It was three and a half years of living through, as Sharma says, 'The Perfect Storm'.

Tehelka.com had exposed the defense deal scandal a few days after the budget of 2001. The sting operation showed political leaders taking bribes from fake arms dealers. The sting operation was a huge loss of face for the ruling party, Bhartiya Janta Party (BJP), as its President, Bangaru Laxman, was seen on camera taking one lakh rupees.

As the BJP-led government came under fire, so did Sharma, ostensibly for his role in the bear cartel. But he says that it became clear during the hundreds of times he was interrogated that the State was after him for his investment in the news portal.

Sharma's home and offices were raided twenty-six times. All eighteen branch offices had to be closed down. Sharma was banned from trading on the stock exchange. He had to lay off three hundred employees. And it did not end there.

Sharma was jailed for nearly two months. He was kept with terrorists and murderers in Tihar jail in Delhi and Arthur Road jail in Mumbai. Between 2001 and 2004, Sharma was summoned to court about three hundred times. He spent seventy-four days in jail for an alleged FERA violation—for not taking the RBI's permission before doing business with FIIs.

'It was a nightmare and could have never ended if the ruling government would not have gone out of power.'

Sharma's life turned inside out as *Tehelka*'s sting operation showed several political figures as well as army top brass, colluding to take bribes to approve defence contracts. Sharma was a principal investor with a 14.5 percent stake in *Tehelka*. He was sent to Jail without bail under a law that had been repealed a year and a half earlier by the Parliament. He received three hundred summons from various agencies and departments of the government, including the Income Tax Department, the Enforcement Directorate, the Excise Department, the Department of Company Affairs, and the Reserve Bank of India.

'If it would have gone on for ten years, we wouldn't have survived.'

'It was right from the top, not even one guy in the establishment stood up. Each one of them was a puppet. Goolam Essaji Vahanvati (current Attorney General of India) was the only one who stood up. That was the real awakening. These guys could kill you,' he says.

'When you invest in business, you don't think your life will be taken away. I didn't budget for that. It wasn't even a big investment.'

'There were moments when I wanted to walk away. When the pressure was just so much—the Government of India has a million ways to get to you.'

However, Sharma fought in every possible way. He stayed in the game and read up all that he could on laws and acts that were being raised against him. After the first raid by Income Tax officials, Sharma went and bought books on 'Search and Seizure'. He counterquestioned the Income Tax authorities since he realized he had to be proactive in this fight and not reactive. He anticipated the next move and did everything to be prepared for it.

The realization didn't come as quickly though. Initially, every move by the government agencies tracking his every move came as a shock and a new learning—like the time he was taken from his home to the police station on the pretext of recording his statement on an allegation by an Income Tax officer. It was only when he was in the car, which was not a police jeep, but a close friend's car, that he was told he was getting arrested.

'We fought at all levels. Middle-class professionals don't realize that law is open to interpretation. We understood that.'

Sharma and Mehra both had middle-class sensibilities; their family's biggest investment was in educating them. Devina Mehra is a gold medalist from the Indian Institute of Management, Ahmedabad and Sharma, an MBA from the Asian Institute of Management, Manila. Sharma and Mehra didn't have any political godfathers or a network to tap into for help. They had completely focussed on building their capabilities as individuals and professions, and that's what they knew they could count on.

'We were in our mid-thirties—first-generation entrepreneurs; there was no general template for us. But both Devina and I come from lawless parts of the country. We hail from a family of freedom fighters. That bloodline came to the fore: 'I will not bow to the government.'

In good times, everybody is your friend or wants to be your friend; in bad times, one needs to look within to find that strength, courage, and conviction to carry on. Sharma and Mehra tapped their inner strength and intuition to fight back. They thought like them, behaved like them, they only imagined the worse and prepared for the worst. They knew it was a street fight and they had to get their hands dirty.

'Don't think honorably—this is a street fight. In a street fight there are no rules. You have to think like a criminal. You shouldn't hold on to your ideals. You have to think like the enemy. If they trap, you trap them.'

It is usually when we are most vulnerable that we seek advice from almost everyone. We try to find solutions to our problems from the experiences and advice of others. However, Sharma and Mehra took the contrarian path. When advice from all quarters, including friends, family, including their lawyers, was to keep a low profile and essentially not be seen or heard much, Sharma and Devina Mehra fought a high decibel campaign. They gave media interviews, held press conferences, putting their story out there seemed like the only way forward. They communicated relentlessly and passionately, always highlighting the wrong done to them.

Sharma worked with the legal team round-the-clock. It was his fight which he fought with every attention to detail. He did not leave it just to the lawyers; he nearly became a lawyer himself. 'You have to be humble and empower yourself with knowledge—with that you can counter things head-on.'

It was war, and Sharma played every possible move not written in the book. 'It was a complete military operation. We were purely equipped from a knowledge perspective. We educated ourselves overnight.'

Sharma was not always confident that he will be able to see the end of this. Perhaps, it was that fear that kept him motivated. 'Confidence is not good enough. Too much confidence is just bravado.'

Ultimately Sharma was given a clean chit; a change of administration at the Centre helped.

Nearly a decade later, Sharma is back in business. He has rebuilt his business again; reopened offices, got the clients and his credibility back.

Also, he says, he has structured his life in a way that it won't be as easy to 'get to him' this time.

He has given up his Indian residency, has diversified his assets across the world, and has decided to never invest in media stocks. He and Devina Mehra have also started a new venture, Cerebra Brain Tech Pvt. Ltd. The technology- and research-based venture seeks to enhance mental capabilities as well as provide solutions for neurological disorders like autism, alzheimer's, depression, and schizophrenia.

'Just be knowledgeable about the game you are playing, you don't have to be honourable. If the guy is sleeping, by all means go and kill him—don't think the battle is from nine to five,' says the battle-scarred Sharma.

WHY I FAILED

- I did not understand the extent to which the government could go after you
- I made a wrong investment decision that took my life away

Advice

- When in war, think like the enemy
- Knowledge and effective communication can be your best tools in a crisis
- Don't be intimidated. Fight back
- In a battle or a war, don't think of ideals
- One should work with the assumption that the state's intentions are always dishonourable and suspect

Acknowledgements

I had no idea when I started working on this project how much fun and how challenging writing on failure would be. Nobody really likes to talk about failure—it's a word that can get the most successful and confident be edgy, nervous, and wary. Every discussion on the subject would raise eyebrows, explanations would be sought, advice would be given and automatically the conversation would steer towards more 'interesting' topics.

Well, here I am, years later, putting together my list of people who made this project happen. It was Chiki Sarkar who plucked me out of nowhere and convinced me that I could really do it. I am likewise very grateful to my editors at Random House, Radhika Marwah and Milee Ashwarya, who were as enthusiastic as they were patient. This book would not have happened without your support.

I am also very thankful to the editor of *Business Today*, Chaitanya Kalbag, whose advice and thought-provoking questions helped me probe my own feelings about failure.

I wouldn't have been able to write this book if it hadn't been for all those who agreed to speak to me about their experiences; and they did so with tremendous generosity and insight. I want to express my gratitude to all those people who opened up to share their stories and in the process helped me grow and learn—Abhinav Bindra, Anu Aga, Sminu Jindal, Narayana Murthy, Madhur Bhandarkar, Subhash Ghai, Ajit Gulabchand, Sunil Alagh, Sanjiv Goenka, Sabyasachi Mukherjee, Kiran Mazumdar-Shaw, Captain Gopinath, Shankar Sharma, Prathap Reddy, William Bissell, and Narayanan Vaghul—each of their stories have been an inspiration.

Then there were those people who were always around, and whose presence, support and advice I have always taken for granted. They were generous with their thoughts, ideas, patience, humour, and support.

Hindol Sengupta: For his constant encouragement and belief in me. My sounding board for a lot of the ideas and thoughts that have shaped this book

Aarti Bagdi: For her unmatched enthusiasm which kept me going during the most trying times

Kakuni Mahto: My oldest friend, who has always been by my side

Pooja Chandra: For saying it as it is, for painstakingly plucking through every sentence and pulling me up at every slip

A few people deserve special thanks, much, much more than I know how to express.

Surinder Mohan, Kaushalya, and Bimla: For their love and the most endearing stories that shape my world today

Shashi and Balbir Punj: For everything there is and ever will be

Sourabh Tripathi: For being the calm voice of reason in my very chaotic world

Mansi Punj: For sharing my many failures

Ahaana Aggarwal: For the immense joy and perspective she has brought into my life

Tarini and Prakash Tripathi: For their unwavering support and encouragement in everything I do

And, finally my son Aarav, who makes me see poetry in the mundane. For his toothless smiles, chuckles, and coos that kept me going through the many times when all I wanted to do was just get some sleep.

In a way, this book, has been as much about writing about failure as experiencing it. There have been hits and misses. There have been moments of immense agony and complete joy. There have been times of crippling self-doubt and fleeting moments of unbelievable confidence—overall—it's been a cathartic journey and I am grateful to have experienced it.

A Note on the Author

Shweta is a business journalist, a television host, and a social entrepreneur. She is associate editor at *Business Today*. She has worked for more than a decade in India and the US reporting on business and policy for a wide variety of organizations including CNBC TV18, Inside Washington Publishers, Bloomberg UTV, and NewsX. A two-part series authored by her on outsourcing was nominated for the 'Best Business Story Award-North America'. She is also the co-founder of the New Delhi-based research think tank The Whypoll Foundation which runs India's first public service and governance feedback social networking domain www. whypoll.org.

ADVANCE PRAISE FOR THE BOOK

'Success and failure go hand in hand in the life of every person. The lessons one learns from failures provide the foundation to build a success story. In India, we fear failure and thereby success becomes a distant dream. We need to honour and celebrate ideas and people who fail, for they are the ones who are best prepared to script their successes. Shweta's book on learnings from failure is a marvelous effort and a must read for anyone who wants to achieve something big.'

—**Kishore Biyani**, Founder and Group CEO, Future Group

'In my professional life as an entrepreneur, I have had experiences of both success and failure. Without being disheartened, I had the courage of conviction to learn from failures to build further success. Shweta has provided a fairly good insight into lessons learnt from events of failure, which will certainly help readers immensely.'

—**Dr Vijay Mallya**, Chairman, UB Group

'In an era of sanitized books on successes, Shweta Punj has a very unusual take – how we can learn from our failures. These vignettes from 16 leaders will greatly benefit anyone who wants to go beyond uplifting stories, to really learning from those who have tried, failed and finally succeeded.'

—**Nandan Nilekani**, Chairman, Unique Identification Authority of India and co-founder of Infosys Ltd

'Success and failure are the two inextricably interwoven aspects of life. While success is celebrated, failure is forgotten and often despised. Shweta Punj has broken trodden tradition and has dealt with 'failure' in an immaticulate style. While those who fail surely learn from their mistakes, the book gives an opportunity to all of us to benefit from the unhappy experiences of others. The book has been written in a racy style and makes an interesting and take away read.'

—**G.N. Bajpai**, Former Chairman, Securities and Exchange Board of India